SEXUAL MADNESS

In a Sexually Confused World

By Dr. Alan Pateman

BY DR. JENNIFER PATEMAN

AVAILABLE FROM APMI PUBLICATIONS, AMAZON.COM AND OTHER RETAIL OUTLETS

Drs. ALAN & JENNY

SEXUAL MADNESS

PATEMAN

BOOK TITLE:

SEXUAL MADNESS: In a Sexually Confused World

WRITTEN BY Drs. ALAN & JENNY PATEMAN
ISBN: 978-1-909132-02-3
eBook ISBN: 978-1-909132-03-0

Published By:
APMI Publications
In Partnership with Truth for the Journey Books **5**
Email: publications@alanpateman.com
www.AlanPatemanMinistries.com

Acknowledgements:
Author/Design/Senior Editor/Publisher: Apostle Dr. Alan Pateman
Editing/Proofreading/Research: Dr. Jennifer Pateman
Computer Administration/Office Manager: Dr. Dorothea Struhlik
Cover Image Credit: www.PosterMyWall.com

Unless otherwise indicated, Scripture quotations are from the King James Version of the bible.

Where scriptures appear with special emphasis (in bold, italic or underlined) we have edited them ourselves in order to bring focused attention within the context of this subject being taught.

❖

Dedication

We dedicate this book to true *SEXUAL LIBERTY* that can only come through the teachings of Jesus Christ.

❖

Table of Contents

❖

Foreword

Liberty is a fluid concept today. What one man calls freedom is another man's bondage. The definition of "normal" is open to every kind of interpretation and the fear of "offending" in the public arena has reached new levels.

Our rights are crumbling in the name of *political correctness*. Even the differences in meaning between **tolerance** and **acceptance** have blurred to the point of no return. Emotional, sexual and spiritual confusion governs!

In the absence of a true **moral compass** we have reaped decay. Right and wrong - as opposite as the polar icecaps - cannot reverse themselves. If we dictate their natural order should change, then the world would drop off its axis and spin out of control. *(Out of shape and out of balance - much like today's present reality!)*

Yet in my ministry I seek to love people of all shapes, sizes, race and creed, including sexual orientation. But so too do I stand unswervingly towards the truth, which unlike popular opinion is NOT subject to change. *(It is neither interchangeable nor replaceable!)*

Even though it's no longer present within our schools, courts of law, hospitals or other public arenas, the bible still has never lost its POWER *(or ability to OFFEND!)* And sharper contrasts are continually being drawn: politically, socially, religiously, and every other conceivable way - that will unquestionably force people to make a *stance,* one-way or the other.

As for me and my house we will serve the Lord!
(Joshua 24:15)

❖

Introduction

It has been our intention during the writing of this particular book to bring clarification to *sexuality* without condemning anybody.

Many today are saying that marriage has moved on or evolved and should therefore include other orientations. As a result *same-sex-marriages* are on the rise and many Christians are beginning to accept this concept in an attempt to be seen as *tolerant* and *loving*.

However even though Jesus ate with and showed love to the prostitutes He still told them to, *"Go and sin no more!"* This means that He loved people, without loving their life styles. Nor was He afraid to call sin - *SIN!*

Today we are frightened to label anything as sin, in case we might offend someone. But the truth *does* offend and it also liberates. The offense is a necessary reaction, but how we hate the conflict. We prefer peace at the cost of peace!

To this effect people are currently changing their worldviews purely for sentimental reasons. For example they are willing to replace correct theology for wrong theology just because they met someone who was in blatant sin but who was also *"a very nice person!"* However this is NOT adequate premise for *replacement theology,* as this spiritual battle we face is not a personality contest. The struggle is a spiritual one and never a personal one.

Many things can feel so right and be so wrong! That's why it's dangerous to accept anything just on the basis that it *feels* good. Nothing can automatically be right, just because our emotions say so. Sentiments change with the wind but TRUTH endures forever, regardless of our flesh, emotions and popular opinion.

We cannot turn in ignorance from the facts, hoping they'll go away! For never before has teen suicide been so high. Never before have authorities considered teaching homosexuality, transgender issues and cross-dressing to six year olds or seen the need to define *orientations* such as *sadomasochism* through illustrated textbooks. Never before have so many young people needed psychiatric assistance.

The list is longer but the only thing that can sustain life - spirit soul and body - creating a healthy *balance* from the inside out, is the living Word of God.

Therefore we have written this book to encourage people into *freedom, balance, faith and a relationship with the Lord Jesus Christ, by and through the power of the Holy Spirit,* whose soaking presence is able to convict us of the truth. Only by living and walking with the Spirit and Truth in this way, can we truly avoid all that is false.

Even though a very real battle wages for our minds, we are convinced that this book will help take you on a journey of discovery that will help you and all those you speak with. God who has instigated this book - will continue working in your life - long after you put this book down.

We promise you that there *IS* true freedom in Christ, which can be yours right now if you will just believe. God is on your side and nothing is too difficult for Him.

So take great courage...
We are routing for you!

Doctors Alan & Jenny Pateman

CHAPTER 1

Sex Education

As I was thinking about this book, my 15 year old son came into my office and told me how the girls in his class were constantly talking about sex and who they are having it with *(14-15 year old girls)*. He added, "Dad in my class, when it comes to sex... the girls are the worst!"

This speaks volumes, although it is not so "shocking" anymore, sadly enough. People come to expect it and are numb to the realities and consequences of such rampant promiscuity.

In addition to this, my son informed me that during his "Sexual Education Classes" all students were *encouraged* to go home and do *homework* on the subject - via the Internet! This spells TROUBLE straight away. As it doesn't take a genius to know that when a teenager *(or anyone)* types the word "SEX" into their browser, PORNOGRAPHY will be the result! This ensures that entire generations of youngsters are exposed to *hard-core-pornography* at the very behest of their teachers - how utterly bizarre.

I advise "ALL" parents to monitor and supervise their children when it comes to computer access. There is a plethora of family-protective-software and accountability-programs available. *(There's simply no doubt that the Internet affects ALL age groups and such programs can help safeguard the entire family).* As my son pointed out, this phenomenon does not just influence boys. It is fact that female teenagers are also very promiscuous indeed.

In fact all over the world young people who are just *setting-out* in life, are heavily encouraged to *fornicate*. Many avenues exist such as the TV, peer pressure at school, radio, the MTV culture, contemporary lyrics and most of today's advertising campaigns. All of which thrust the "SEX-NOW" message in their young faces!

Using such arguments as, "Forget abstinence and withholding yourself for marriage, this is old fashioned and archaic, be free and express your natural animal instincts instead. Conservatism is BONDAGE. Be *liberal;* be *normal* and stop being *frigid!* Flow with the chemistry and HAVE SEX NOW... what are you waiting for? Go with the urge; ignore your conscience - that's only for nuns! Enjoy your youth as you only live once. THROW AWAY RESTRAINT and have sex whenever, wherever and with whomsoever. If it feels right, then it *must* be right - just be safe!"

Notice that the only *responsibility* they attach to this spin *(sexual propaganda)* is the use of contraception! Suggesting that safety includes equipping oneself with the latest, most colourful and scented condoms everywhere one goes! So what does this leave us with? Well it has to be said, that in today's world, if a school leaver, leaves school with no other qualifications, they have at least learnt how to have SAFE SEX!

Such is the legacy that we are leaving our youth. Such are the warped set of priorities that are being taught to our following generations. It could be said like this, that our youth today are so WELL INFORMED about sex, that they have really been taught and shown how to go about it!

Okay so young horny-teenagers hardly need any encouragement in these matters and if no one talked about it in the schools, no one is really saying they wouldn't get up to it anyway - for sure they would. But, while some are more than ready to indulge their senses and get home tutoring on the subject; there are still others who are just NOT ready. For this reason we MUST ask the question, **"Are we allowing our youngest and dearest to be introduced to the world of sex before their time?"**

God wants you to live a pure life. Keep yourselves from sexual promiscuity.

(1 Thessalonians 4:3)

Satan cleverly uses the *trusted* school system, to cunningly seduce the young out of their innocent ignorance into full blown promiscuity by informing and convincing them in a sophisticated and educated manner that it's okay because TIMES HAVE CHANGED!

They are told, "Progressive thinking means that you can make educated decisions of your own without the influence of religion. Such traditions and fundamentalist views only *stifle* your freedom. While proper information helps you reduce the risks and take the right precautions. Go ahead and give up your most precious commodity - virginity! Do it in spite of religion, parents and old ways of thinking. Be modern."

Evidently through the guise of EDUCATION we have allowed our youth to be encouraged into sexual activity - whether they're ready or not - deleting the natural sense of "caution" or "fear" that most young people have about sex. Without healthy encouragement for sexual-restraint, our young and innocent are cleverly being prepared *(not for the Gospel)* for ABUSE!

But some would defend the current situation with the argument, "Leave them alone, don't you realize that your legalism is the problem here - lighten up!" Suggesting that our fundamental views are legalistic. By no means! True fundamentals stand for FREEDOM. Including sexual freedom. God wants us to enjoy sex. Yes ENJOY it! It was created for our pleasure *(1 Timothy 6:17b)* and was a marriage gift from God for the married couple. A GIFT to be opened on the wedding night not before! Opened at its rightful time, then fully enjoyed and kept sacred before God.

Consider it this way; God could have chosen to give us no pleasure out of sex at all. Making it a *needs-must* exercise that is totally *necessity-driven* and void of all pleasure instead. *Endured* rather than *enjoyed* simply to ensure the on-going population of the world! However the fact remains that God did NOT do things that way, which proves something rather vivid about His divine nature. That **He took our pleasure and quality of life into consideration and made it one of His chief concerns!**

I know that I may be labouring the point here a little, but the word *pleasure* has often been viewed in a negative light, even though God Himself created it, on every conceivable level for all of our five senses to enjoy! However the extreme always exists and scripture warns us about people worshiping pleasure rather than its creator.

We see this directly in 2 Timothy 3:4 where it says, *"... men shall be lovers of their own selves... unthankful... **lovers of pleasures rather than lovers of God.**"* How often does humanity stop to marvel at the beauty of nature, with all its scenic views and forget to accredit its divine artist? Of whom 1 Timothy 6:17 speaks, *"...the living God, who giveth us richly all things to enjoy."* Including John 10:10 where it states, *"life more abundantly."*

However, along with pleasure God also provides appropriate "safety-nets," which in the case of sex is marriage; a correct and healthy boundary for proper sexual relations. Yet this image of a perfect God with His perfect provision for our lives gets distorted. As we have said previously, we are sold the lie very early on, that we must gain some experience, before settling for one; a life-partner must be sexually compatible and therefore we must experiment. The problem with this lie of course is when do we STOP experimenting and where do we draw the line?

Instead our youth should be prepared scripturally for life and taught to TRUST the Lord concerning their future *(rather than their sexual appetites!)* He alone can navigate such a type-roped-journey as this. It is in all these things that both young or single people in particular, MUST put their faith and trust fully in God. Deciding that God is ABLE even when it comes to sexual-compatibility of their future partner.

There is no denying it, this requires a rock-solid TRUST and a prayerful willingness to wait until He reveals who, where, when and how. Only Satan is in a hurry and considering you could be marrying heaven or hell - it's worth the wait.

Experimentation and promiscuity only leads to confusion, comparisons, hurts, and a whole host of other obstacles that create heavy baggage for any marriage and robs couples of the God-intended-intimacy for their relationship. In its place they find a poisonous concoction of lust, pain, hurt and abuse that has infiltrated their marriage instead.

Consequently it is vital then that we choose wisely between the SCHOOL OF FORNICATION and the SCHOOL OF THE HOLY SPIRIT for our children! The harvest of fornication is manifold: abuse, hurt, pain, division, divorce, infidelity, child abuse, pornography and illegitimacy. Is this really what we want for our young people - to create a multitude of souls with an ORPHAN SPIRIT and IDENTITY CRISIS?

The book of Revelations 2:20 warns us that Jezebel's intentions won't cease that easily. Even today this spirit actively looks to EDUCATE and ENTICE folks to commit sexual sins... nothing has changed - she still looks *"to teach... fornication [sexual immorality]."*

Now let me add here, that there is a BALANCE TO EVERYTHING and I want to encourage balance at all costs! Teaching our children about sex is NOT wrong! Of course it's not. Although as believers the agenda behind our Sexual-Education is completely different from that of the world. Which is PREPARATION FOR MARRIAGE NOT PROMISCUITY!

I dare say that, as Christian parents we can see that there's a definite LINE to be drawn here! As there's a mighty lot of difference between INFORMING and AIDING-N-ABETTING! I am sure that most parents, Christian or otherwise, once having discussed the delicate subject of sex with their young ones, wouldn't dream of pulling out condoms, showing them how to use them and then giving them a small supply, "TO BE SAFE!" What a confusing signal that would give: like red, green and amber all at once!

❖

CHAPTER 2

Premature Sexualisation

In the last chapter we discussed the subject of TEENAGE PROMISCUITY and the PREMATURE SEXUALISATION of our young people, which violates their intended and rightful time *(Ecclesiastes 3:11)*. Now we will go a little deeper still, to further unveil the irony of this subject. That the very things set in place to encourage SAFE SEX only cause more vulnerability!

> *To the pure, all things are pure, but to those who are corrupted and do not believe, nothing is pure. In fact, both their minds and consciences are corrupted.*
>
> *(Titus 1:15 NIV)*

Take for instance any young person, who has been encouraged into promiscuity and sexual activity but then commits to become a Christian and eventually marries another Christian. For a while everything seems great, until this same person who once enjoyed such sexual freedom as a former-fornicator, now finds themself experiencing all kinds of sexual HANG-UPS. Past experiences and comparisons haunt their mind, with flashbacks and shameful memories.

In addition now that they are in Christ and should be enjoying the fruit of their right-relations, instead they are discovering that the guilt, shame, pain and condemnation from past events is now effectively hindering the present and SHUTTING-THEM-DOWN to sex. Needless to say that such SHUTTING DOWN sexually only causes this couple great heartache, confusion and frustration.

It's evident then that two basic *lies* prevail. As previously mentioned, the first lie is aimed principally at the single non-Christian, "Forget restraint, live it up while you can!" Then comes the second lie that's aimed at the young and frustrated but married Christian couple! "Pull yourselves together, don't be lustful. Sex is sinful. Show restraint!"

This means that before they knew God, they showed no restraint but once they did know Him, they were expected to show plenty of restraint! This is backward. The time to show restraint is *before* marriage not afterwards! When the fullness of time arrives and marriage takes place, this is precisely when a young couple is meant to enjoy their intimacy.

These lies suggest that SEXUAL FREEDOM is for the sinner but NOT for the saint! Yet true sexual liberty ONLY exists in the teachings of Christ! So listening to either lie robs young people of the beauty and blessing that was intended for sex.

Then in addition to all of this, the young wife gets pushed the idea; "You don't HAVE to have sex whenever HE wants it... who does he think he is anyway? You don't have to submit to him. Don't surrender yourself stop being submissive. Your body is your own NOT his." All of which is directly out of line with scripture, *(see 1 Peter 3:1-7; Ephesians 5:22-33, Colossians 3:18-20).* Simply because the Christian marriage - a couple that have a loving and intimate relationship - **submit to one another in** LOVE *(Ephesians 5:21).*

My wife tends to prefer the Message Bible for the following verses because it helps take the *religion* out of it. So let's take a look at Ephesians 5:21-33,

> *Out of respect for Christ, be courteously reverent to one another. Wives understand and support your husbands... The husband provides leadership to his wife the way Christ does to his church, not by domineering but by cherishing... wives should likewise submit to their husbands. Husbands, go all out in your love for your wives, exactly as Christ did for the church - a love marked by giving, not getting... His words evoke her beauty... that is how husbands ought to love their wives... loving himself in loving her, and how each wife is to honour her husband.*

So the contradiction exists today, that young girls in particular are encouraged to *submit their bodies* when OUTSIDE of marriage but not when IN IT! Take for example the nightclub scene and the bars, where fornication is routine and promiscuity is promoted through the deliberately seductive music and atmosphere. When in such a drunken haze, "submission" is rarely an issue! Many young girls willingly give their bodies up for fornication. They dress and behave provocatively, openly flirting and allowing men of all ages to lust after them.

Let me interject here so that we don't confuse passion with lust. Passion is not lust. Lust is self-gratification, which seeks the fulfilment of one's *own* pleasure rather than seeking to *give* pleasure in a meaningful way to someone special. Sex as God intended it is an expression of love, which is not selfish.

To think that God wants Christians to have passionless sex is sad because sex without passion is dead! Or do we really believe that enjoyment in sex is only intended for the sinner?

This type of thinking obviously convinces many, because the same girls who behave one way in fornication behave the opposite way when married. Is it expected of them? Is it a forced and learnt behaviour that is meant to restrict them and hinder their best interests? Of course!

When they enter marriage this *learnt-behaviour* cannot measure up to the marriage commitment, which is a JOINT and UNSELFISH commitment.

It is an accepted fact today that most young men and women who go to nightclubs and such, go with the intention of having sex. It's taken for granted especially where young women are concerned, that they go "prepared" for sex. Again it's in the way they dress and behave, fuelled with drugs and alcohol to enhance mood and numb inhibitions.

So what is encouraged by the world is now discouraged in marriage. Sexual readiness is suddenly viewed as something "wrong," and sexual spontaneity dwindles. In other words, outside of the drunken haze and nightclub atmosphere, back in the mundane *status-quo* of everyday living - couples find themselves *stifled* and no longer *free* to enjoy sex. ALL THIS MEANS THAT THEY HAVE BEEN SCHOOLED AND PREPARED FOR FORNICATION BUT NOT FOR MARRIAGE.

This parody makes it very difficult for them to make the switch and know how to respond within a different set of boundaries. In fact everything they learn at school undermines the institute of marriage. The big green light for premarital sex and promiscuity sets them up for a fall when it comes to marriage. The agenda? To *destroy* society as we know it.

This applies to all ages of course and not just for the youth of our society, nevertheless we can see that this whole subject is entirely on its head! Upside-down completely, because of an almighty "clash" in interests.

The world says, "BE FREE IN FORNICATION!" While God says, "BE FREE IN MARRIAGE." Yet the truth for many who indulged in fornication before marriage, have considerable difficulty being free after marriage, especially women. The reality is that what the devil calls freedom is really bondage!

Therefore if any man be in Christ, he is a new creature: old things are passed away; behold, all things are become new.
(2 Corinthians 5:17)

However in Christ a person can be totally set free from their past, where old things are PASSED AWAY and all things are become NEW. This includes God's BEST being restored to their lives!

In God we are free. There is no bondage in Christ. An important realization is that while the spirit of this world tells us to have sex without restraint, God also told us not to WITHHOLD ourselves from one another! But within marriage, because this alone provides the correct setting for "safe sex!"

Again the reality is this - everything that the world is seeking for in sex, is available right in the midst of what God ordained. What the world considers "sexual liberation" usually involves much bondage. On the other hand - those who operate in the fullness of what God has ordained for their lives, are the ones who enjoy true freedom!

Now for some folks this is where the struggle BEGINS! The devil has convinced many that it's wrong to be SEXY AND GODLY AT THE SAME TIME! This throws an enormous WET-BLANKET on the subject of sex. However sex was created for pleasure and not for shame, not for guilt and not for regret.

The blessing of the LORD, it makes rich, and he adds NO SORROW *with it.*

(Proverbs 22:10)

Perverting generations before they ever get the chance to enjoy marriage the way God intended, means that Satan can successfully "steal, kill and destroy" their inheritance. He confuses their perception of the Father's highest and best for them in this crucial area.

The serpent's nature is always to seduce and tempt. But it does not stop there. He also indulges in "condemning" and "accusing." His master plan is to "seduce" and to "lure" people into sin - once they respond, led away by their own lust *(see James 1:14)* he proceeds to torment them with the guilt and shame of their own actions...!

As a liar and the father of all lies Satan has always made such a huge deal out of sex. Why? Because it poses such a threat to him and if he can successfully convince us that something **pure is perverse** - this means we can no longer enjoy it. *"Do not call anything impure that God has made clean"* *(Acts 10:15 NIV).*

Conversely if he can convince the world that only "perversity" is enjoyable and purity is boring - then they will happily remain indifferent towards the things of God!

Finally in closing this chapter - there can simply be no mistake - we have been ordained to live a full life! This excludes no area. In Christ we are free in ALL things *(John 8:36).*

The thief comes only to steal and kill and destroy; I have come that they may have life, and have it to the FULL.
                                        (John 10:10 NIV)

❖

CHAPTER 3

The Seduction of Women

Welcome to this third chapter, which is going to cover the seduction of women. In the last two chapters we largely focused on the failure of the school system, to prepare our young people for their futures.

> It is obvious what kind of life develops out of trying to get your own way all the time: repetitive, loveless, cheap sex... If you use your freedom this way, you will not inherit God's kingdom.
>
> (Galatians 5:19-21 MSG)

Now we'll look at what's behind all of this and what is spiritually *fuelling* it. The nature of this subject "warrants" a greater understanding from us, as it affects each and every one of us NOT just the younger generations.

To achieve this *deeper delve* I have taken some teaching from one of my books, that I wrote some years ago entitled "Israel, The Church and The End Times!" Page 128 onwards discusses the spiritual warfare that goes on, which the majority of the church is ignorant about.

There is a New Age war going on, which is mainly targeting "young females," although it promotes all kinds of perversion, including homosexuality *(of which we will discuss in chapter seven).*

Mainly the New Age movement worships "Mother Earth" and of course brings the Catholic Church into its embrace because of the worship of "Madonna" as being the "Mother of all" and the "Creator of all." We can even see how the new age movement has brought this emphasis of "mother-worship" into blockbusters such as **"Avatar."**

The whole theme was to protect Mother Earth *(whom they called "Eywa")* - for instance healing came through her - only if you became one with her. This film cleverly captured hearts due to the love story woven into its theme.

So let us continue and look at this New Age phenomena, Mother goddess, the Sex Queen because according to Wanda Marrs the seduction of women is top priority on Satan's hidden New Age agenda. Her startling book was perhaps one of the first to completely reveal the New Age campaign to deceive and seduce women.

For instance Satan knows that if he can capture the mind and body of a woman, then he can quite easily conquer her husband, children, entire family and circle of friends too!

In her book "New Age Lies to Women," Wanda Marrs thoroughly documents the almost incredible plan of the New Age leadership to foster sexual immorality by inciting lustful feelings and creating seductive imagery in women's minds. She also explains how the New Age has successfully been able to damage and hurt women psychologically, break up marriages, lure our children into Satanism, cults and the occults, kill unborn babies, and undermine women's faith in God.

Wanda says in her book *(p107)* that the Mother Goddess *(Semiramis)* "...was also called the Queen of Heaven. She bedecked herself with jewels and gold and spread the doctrine that those who followed her and were initiated into the 'mysteries' would be prosperous and gain abundant material wealth and enjoy sexual ecstasy as spiritual gifts from gods.

Drunkenness and merriment was a prime feature of worship as revellers lifted their cups and chanted praises to the goddess. Sexual orgies then followed a revealing of the mysteries, the secretive, satanic doctrines that were taught by Babylonian priests and priestesses. Today, the sexual rituals and licentiousness of Babylon are back, introduced into modern-day society by the New Age."

It is interesting that in Italy, a country devoted to the Catholic Church, and committed to the worship of Madonna is also a country steeped in sexual immorality; with pornography and prostitution available everywhere. Not to mention the more recent worldwide scandals involving paedophile priests which was milked by the international media and triggered calls for the resignation of the Pope!

This New Age agenda has been propagated also through the music industry - sexually suggestive and occult scenes, violence, illicit sex and the occult seem to go hand in hand with many rock bands.

"Heavy-metal groups take their listeners even farther out. One group, Judas Priest, on their album, 'Defenders of the Faith,' sang 'Eat Me Alive,' the words depicting a girl being forced at gun point to commit oral sex. Even more explicit are the words of songs by groups like W.A.S.P.

For example, the lyrics of one of their songs spoke of pictures of naked ladies lying on the bed and the smell of sweet convulsion and about howling in heat and finally, about committing the sex act, like a beast" (Rock is a Four Lettered Word, p70).

Another clear example of the negative moulding power of pop idols was the claim by a child-pornography expert. In a report to the United Press International, Judith Reisman said the following:

"Pictures encourage child pornography. You're dealing with an idol or heroine who carries with her a great deal of power and symbolism. For example, Madonna is seen as a desired being in society, so all young women want to be desired; they want to achieve. If the nude pictures in popular magazines are described as appropriate, desirable behaviour, then youngsters, both girls and boys, will construe that to be the case. Large numbers of them will. Thus the pictures will encourage voluntary displays by youngsters. That is not good.

As far as the negative sexual problems, one newsmagazine reported that women all too often are portrayed as 'bimbos'. They undress in silhouette; stretch out over car hoods and snarl like animals. Their dress includes fishnet and leathers" *(Women in a Video Cage, p54).*

At the time of writing my book some ten years ago I included the likes of Madonna. But of course today I can add an array of others who have *progressed* or *regressed* since Madonna's prime - such as Lady Gaga - who also helps PERVERT THE MASSES. However if we looked at Madonna's hit video **"Like a Prayer"** from 1989 it was full of religious imagery and blasphemous overtones. The video began in a church setting as Madonna sensually caressed the feet of a statue of a black Catholic saint.

The icon shed tears and then came to life. She picked up a dagger, touched the blade and the palms of her hands began to bleed, which mimicked the superstition known as "stigmata," *(a supernatural event which many believe signifies God's blessing on an individual).* Madonna then danced in a field of burning crosses, in little more than a slip and was seductively kissed by this "saint" character. There was even a scene that implied lesbian activity, on the church's altar, with a choir member!

The huge advertisements that hung in record stores across America, which peddled the "Like A Prayer, LP" - used the inscription, "Lead Us Not To Temptation." Also the singer went as far as having "Patchouli" *(West Indian fragrance)* mixed in with its packaging glue, **"scented to simulate church incense"** which was a significant marketing technique employed by Madonna. Her publicist, Liz Rosenberg could hardly cover up the stench the video created *(USA Today, March 30th, 1989. PD1)*. Also see http:// en.wikipedia.org/wiki/Like_a_Prayer.

❖

CHAPTER 4

The Naked Truth

So it is true to say that the New Age Movement in particular is *capturing tens of thousands of women's souls* specifically through sexual lies.

Don't be naive. There are difficult times ahead. As the end approaches, people are going to be self-absorbed... profane... addicted to lust, and allergic to God. They'll make a show of religion, but behind the scenes they're animals.

(2 Timothy 3:4 MSG)

Sex, of course, is a big "draw" throughout society as a whole. Sexual images and erotic fantasies saturate our world. We cannot turn on our television sets or open the pages of a newspaper or woman's magazine without coming face-to-face today with the graphic nature of sexual enticements and inducements. The New Age has mastered the art of inciting lust and unbridled passion in the heart of women.

Wanda Marrs says *(p57-60)*, "This is a religion that has as its core the same unholy practices that were prevalent in Babylon, Egypt, Rome, Greece and throughout the orient. In the centuries before Christ, and in the first centuries after Jesus' first coming, history is replete with the story and descriptions of the fertility rites and the sexual favors granted by the high priestesses in the temple of such cities as Corinth, Athens, Ephesus and Memphis.

Initiates celebrated the sex act with temple prostitutes, **many of whom came from the aristocratic class - from the very cream of society.** In Ephesus and elsewhere, the cult of Diana encouraged sexual license and sacred promiscuity. The idolatrous state of Diana depicted her with a multitude of breasts, signifying her sensual nature. In Egypt, the sensual nature of the mother Goddess, Isis, was also worshipped in fertility rites.

Hislop wrote that, 'Semiramis, the Babylonian **Queen of Heaven** led a licentious life and gave birth to many illegitimate children. Yet, the people grew to worship her as the **Holy Virgin.** In the Goddess religions, it was thought that sacred and ritual sex cleansed and purified; therefore the term **'virgin'** was used, though its meaning is obviously far different than that envisioned by Christians.'

The Roman emperors Nero and Caligula, who professed belief in Roman gods derived from the mystery cults of Babylon and Pergamos, were given to sexual orgies and incredible acts of debauchery and sexual depravity. **Homosexuality and pederasty** *(child abuse)* **was rampant throughout the Roman Empire and especially in Greece were the normal practice of heterosexuality** *(male-female)* **was even sneered at by many of the affluent class and nobility.**

Remembering that the New Agers who practice Tantric yoga actually believe that sexual union - in or out of marriage - bring spiritual communion with the divine energy forces of the universe. Those involved in witchcraft and Satanism consecrated themselves to Satan through ritual sex orgies.

Marilyn Fergusion, in the New Age classic "The Aquarian Conspiracy," enthusiastically reported that, 'For many New Agers, sex outside of marriage is the wave of the future.' She also said that, 'The traditional view of fidelity, *one man - one woman,* has given way to more *liberated* views.' Quoting sociological experts, Ferguson adds that, **'The New Age generation is free from guilt over sex!'**

Promotion Flyer, "1987 International Seth Seminar," Seth an international network of groups composed of disciples of 'Seth,' a demon, channelled by psychic Jane Roberts. This demon taught that, 'the universe is of good intent; evil and destruction does not exist... we create our own reality - literally - through the beliefs we hold, and therefore can change what we don't like.'

In a leaflet published by the Seth Centre, the group stated its main ideas regarding sex as follows:

We are in this to enjoy ourselves - spirit, mind and body.
If it isn't fun, stop doing it...! It is natural to be bisexual.

Heterosexuality, homosexuality and lesbianism are equally worthwhile and valid sexual orientations... There is no authority superior to the guidance of a person's inner self.

Miriam Starhawk and her "Church of Wicca" *(witchcraft)* no doubt agree with the followers of Seth. Starhawk's views of sexuality exactly parallel the wicked doctrines and fertility ritual of the Babylonian mystery cults. Among these decadent views is the astonishingly depraved idea that sexual license is godly. Starhawk expresses this view as follows:

Sexuality is sacred because it is a sharing of energy, in passionate surrender to the power of the goddess, immanent in our desires. In orgasm we share in the force that moves the stars.

Starhawk teaches that witchcraft is the same as the Goddess religion. 'The goddess,' she says, 'is the liberator... and her service is complete freedom.' She also emphasises, the connection for today's New Age woman with the sexuality of the goddess:

The naked body represents truth... the law of the goddess is love: passionate sexual love... The love of the goddess is unconditional... Any act based on love and pleasure is a ritual of the goddess. Her worship can take any form and occur anywhere: it requires no liturgy, no cathedrals, and no confessions."

All this is a far cry from the truth, in fact the bible makes it quite clear in Galatians 5:19-21 that those who indulge in: *"sexual immorality, impurity and debauchery; idolatry and witchcraft; hatred, discord, jealousy, fits of rage, selfish ambition, dissensions, factions and envy; drunkenness, orgies, and the like... will not inherit the kingdom of God"* (NIV).

The following is an excerpt taken from an article written by Robert Eady called **"Satanism, Witchcraft and Church Feminists"** *(Christian Order,* www.catholicculture.org*):*

Wicca & The Catholic Church: Straightforward Wicca or the similar but theologically more ambiguous "Woman-Church" have moved into many areas of the Catholic Church through feminist theologians, feminist-inspired local activists and disgruntled nuns. These Church feminists prey on weak or unorthodox bishops who in turn naively try to involve them in a Church they despise...

Two of the most influential "Catholic-Wiccans" or "Woman-Church" figures to be found opposing the Church are Mary Daly and Rosemary Radford Ruether. **Ex-nun Mary Daly taught lesbian witchcraft.** She has written several books, including the anti-male and anti-Catholic **"Beyond God the Father"** and **"Wickedary,"** a dictionary of sorts for witches.

Dr Rosemary Radford Ruether, an influential speaker and writer who authored **"Sexism and God-Talk,"** was named to the overtly pro-abortion Catholics for the "Free Choice" board back in 1985. In true gnostic style, Reuther described the patriarchal Church as an **"idol of masculinity to be broken up and ground into powder."**

Typical of most "Woman-Church" feminists, Ruether has no problem defying Church teaching on homosexuality. In 1985, when promoting her soon-to-be-released "Women-Church: Theology and Practice of Feminist Liturgical Communities," Ruether promised a feminist - largely Catholic audience - that one chapter would contain liturgies for healing from painful experiences such as coming-out as a lesbian. **"Not that being a lesbian is unnatural, but that the way we've been repressed by homophobia is unnatural."**

At this same gathering she urged participants to establish female "Base Communities," "Women-Church Groups," or "Covens."

So as we can see there is much deception at large and one of Satan's chief priorities is to pervert the role of women, not only in the Church but also in the world in general. He achieves this through seduction and many other forms of deception; sex being one of the most prominent tools that he uses in his hostility against women.

We know from the beginning that Satan has had a hatred for women; *"GOD told the serpent: Because you've done this, you're cursed, cursed beyond all cattle and wild animals, cursed to slink on your belly and eat dirt all your life. I'm declaring war between you and the Woman, between your offspring and hers. He'll wound your head, you'll wound his heel" (Genesis 3:15 MSG).*

❖

CHAPTER 5

Goddess Religion

I n this chapter, including the one directly following this, we are going to be looking at some more statistics centred on the "demand-for" and "consumption-of" - pornography.

Run from sexual sin! No other sin so clearly affects the body as this one does. For sexual immorality is a sin against your own body. Don't you realize that your body is the temple of the Holy Spirit, who lives in you and was given to you by God? You do not belong to yourself, for God bought you with a high price. So you must honour God with your body.

(1 Corinthians 6:18-20 NLT)

For sexuality in general *(irrespective of orientation)* is high on the devil's agenda for the culmination of this age. In fact

PAGANISM as it existed in centuries gone by is still prevalent today - promoting sexual debauchery and intensifying its depravity. So let's take a look at what Wanda Marrs says about this particular subject, "The Goddess & Feminist Catholicism."

To begin with she says *(p143-145)*, "The extent to which the Goddess Religion of the New Age has penetrated many Christian Churches and pseudo - Christian Churches is remarkable, if not astonishing. Its invasion is especially notable.

To their credit, some Catholics themselves are very alarmed at the chain of events now occurring. In the conservative Catholic magazine **"Fidelity"** some time ago was a fascinating and revealing article, **"The Goddess Goes to Washington"** in which Donna Steichen reported that in Washington, D.C, some 2500 people met for a **"Women in the Church"** conference. Most were nuns many of whom were clad in their habits and their veils. **'The conference was an incredible event, a gala that affirmed the coming Goddess Religion!'**

It appeared to be the consensus of the 2500 Catholic nuns, priests, educators and theologians present, that Christianity needs to be **'corrected'** by incorporating the Mother Goddess and her rituals within its institutions. One Catholic sister, Madonna Kolbenschlag, gave a blistering address to the conference. She encouraged the participants, **'in the name of our elder brother Jesus'** to **'be a scandal to the current system of Christianity which promotes the MALE God!'**

'The myth of the Father God,' said Sister Kolbenschlag, 'is largely a product of the Judeo Christian tradition. The Holy One who is truth is beyond all images.' According to Nun Kolbenschlag, whose address was widely and enthusiastically received by the audience, 'the male God of Christianity is a false God who has created the world we live in!'

'It is therefore necessary,' she urged, 'to create a spirituality of a different kind... we must recreate a *new myth* of God.' She then called for a return to the ancient 'Goddess religion.' What she really desired was a combining of the Goddess and the God into one and went on to say, 'Women are clearly the catalyst for the formation of the new spirituality. It is women above all who are in the process of reversing Genesis, turning the myth on its head - and freeing their sexuality.' Finally, to cheers and applause she trumpeted this conclusion: 'The Holy One is breaking through the consciousness of humanity - as the Goddess.'

The priests who assembled at this conference commended the female speakers. Bishop Francis Murphy, Auxiliary of Baltimore, stated, 'They are brilliant women.' Murphy said, 'The Church has to incorporate a lot of modern insights.' Such men as Bishop Francis Murphy and Father David Power and the other male leaders present were not at all embarrassed with the proceedings. They did not even blink when Sister Kolbenschlag remarked, 'Women have always experienced the inner connection of sexuality, affectivity, religious zeal, and the creative impulse. And so we have to ignore the great lie that denies this.'

Another Catholic theologian prominent in the Goddess movement is Matthew Fox. In his book, **"The Coming of the Comic Christ."** Fox wrote that, **'the Christian Church is dying. It is dying because it has rejected the 'Mother-principle.'** Fox continued to say, **'though we love her** *(the Church)* **dearly we should let her die.'** Fox envisions a new church being born today out of the rubble of the Christian Churches, a church that will gloriously uplift the Mother, the Goddess and the feminine principle. **'It's necessary'** he wrote, **'that we all become our Mother's keeper. Mother earth can be awakened;'** he assures us, **'though her pain is great now.'"**

At this point it is easy to see where SPIRITUALITY and SEXUALITY get all mixed up. The following statistics showcase the increase of sexuality right across the board, *(in and outside of the Church)* as a result.

Concerning the following statistics however, the various companies who do the necessary *math* behind such statistics - centring on the DEMAND FOR and the CONSUMPTION OF pornography - take considerable time compiling their information. Therefore statistics can alter relatively quickly in between time - so bear this in mind as you read the general figures represented below - undoubtedly they will have increased significantly! Nevertheless - separated by a handful of years - these statistics are still staggering and give a glimpse into the *enormity* of the problem and porn industry in general.

These figures are compiled by various credible sources such as NEWS and RESEARCH organizations and provide us with proof that porn in today's world is virtually *unavoidable*. Despite the fact that many folks do genuinely land on porn sites by *mistake* it is not the excuse everyone can use, especially "repeat-users, sexual-predators and sex-addicts."

Pornography-Time-Statistics

- Every second $3,075,64 is being spent on pornography.
- Every second 28,258 Internet users are viewing pornography. In that same second 372 Internet users are typing in adult search terms into search engines.
- Every 39 minutes a new pornographic video is being created in the U.S.
- It is big business. The pornography industry has larger revenues than Microsoft, Google, Amazon, eBay, Yahoo, Apple, and Netflix combined.
- For example in 2006 worldwide pornography revenues ballooned to $97.06 billion.

Whatever way we look at this topic, pornography is an ever-growing phenomenon, which is creating as many "sexual-predators" as "sexual-victims." It is an epidemic of our era. **The saddest and most disturbing of all statistics are those that specifically involve the violation of children.**

In closing this chapter we must consider 1 Corinthians 6:18-20 once again and very carefully because most folks don't realize that committing sexual sins, violates their own bodies. It also influences the future because successive generations always end up reaping the consequences.

❖

CHAPTER 6

Porn Consumption

From more recent studies it can quickly be determined that certain places "consume" more pornography than others. Take for instance the nationwide study that took place in the US not so long ago, which revealed how "conservatives" were proven the biggest consumers of porn!

We saw this in an online article written by Ewen Callaway entitled **"Porn in the USA: Conservatives are Biggest Consumers,"** back in February 2009 where he looked into the nationwide study that took place in USA of anonymous credit-card receipts from a major online adult entertainment provider that found little variation in consumption between states. However Benjamin Edelman from Harvard Business School said of the study, **"When it comes to adult entertainment, it seems people are more the same than different."**

The study found that there were some trends to be observed in the data that they compiled - for instance, **"those particular States that consumed the most porn tended to be more conservative and religious than those states with the lower levels of consumption."** Edelman went on to say, **"Some of the people, who are most outraged, turn out to be consumers of the very things that they claimed to be outraged by!"**

It is interesting that after checking for differences between States, he quickly found the differences between them - those with the most adult-purchases and those with the fewest. One discovery he made was that, **"Church goers bought less online porn on Sundays, but expenditures on other days of the week came in line with the rest of the country!"** Such as the residents of the 27 States that passed laws banning gay marriages - who boasted 11% more porn subscribers than those states who don't explicitly restrict gay marriage!

While he continued looking at the associations between "social attitudes" and "pornography consumption" Edelman discovered that particular States in America, where a majority of its residents agreed with the statement: **"I have old-fashioned values about family and marriage,"** actually bought 3.6 more subscriptions per thousand people than States where a majority disagreed! Edelman's final hypothesis for such was REPRESSION saying that, **"If you're told you can't have something, you want it more!"**

Statistics continue; as we have seen already in this book, Satan specifically targets women. His chief motive and plan is to "steal, kill and destroy" ALL of humanity. He is a strategist who understands precisely that if he is capable of subverting the female *(Eve - whose name is life-giver, mother of all living)* he can effectively sway everyone else in the process.

Women are great influencers and have a great deal of power. Satan knows this and wants to pervert and warp it. To do this successfully he must distort, corrupt and misrepresent everything that a WOMAN is meant to be. Depraving and spoiling her destroys the God given and rightful power of influence that she possesses.

So as already stated, *young* ladies in particular today, are proving to be increasingly "hyper-sexual" and "excessively-promiscuous" at a very young age.

In an article called "Women and Pornography" by Jerry Ropelato from the site "Internet Pornography Statistics - Top Ten REVIEWS" this is what he said. "According to stats, men are not the only ones to access pornography at work.

One in three visitors to Pornographic Websites are Women

- Women keeping their cyber activities secret - 70%
- Women struggling with pornography addition - 17%
- Ratio of women to men favouring chat rooms - 2x
- Percentage of visitors to adult websites who are women - 1 in 3
- Women accessing adult websites each month - 9.4 million
- Women admitting to accessing pornography at work - 13%"

He finishes with this bold statement: **"Women, far more than men, are likely to act out their behaviours in real life, such as having multiple partners, casual sex or affairs."**

There are so many official places where these types of statistics can be found. Another site called **"Statistics on Pornography, Sexual Addiction and Online Perpetrators - Pornography addiction Stats/Pornography and Industry Statistics,"** had the following information. *(Note: for lack of space or room to cover all of these statistics, I will mention only a limited amount):*

- According to the *"Internet Filter Review"* in 2006 the total porn industry revenue was $13.3 billion in the US; $97 billion worldwide; also 1 billion adult DVD/ video rentals.
- More shocking to discover was that there are 72 million "unique" worldwide users visiting adult web sites monthly according to the *"Internet Filter Review."* In other words "new" users... Something that will have accelerated since this study took place and is something genuinely "alarming." Satan's agenda to steal kill and destroy is impacting our: cultures, societies and populations from the very "inside-out." Perversion infiltrates our world from every angle.
- The number of hard-core pornography titles released in 2005 *(US):* 13,588 *(Internet Filter Review).*
- More than 70% of men from 18-34 visit a pornographic site in a typical month *(comScore Media Metrix).*
- More than 20,000 images of child pornography posted online every week *(National Society for the Prevention of Cruelty to Children, 10/8/03).*

- Approximately 20% of all Internet pornography involves children *(National Centre for Mission & Exploited Children).*
- 100,000 websites offer illegal child pornography *(U.S. Customs Service estimate).*
- As of December 2005, child pornography was a $3 billion annual industry *(Internet Filter Review).*

Official statistics exist, that specifically reveal the consumption of pornography by Christians, Pastors and Churchgoers. Take for instance the "Promise Keepers" survey that was conducted at one of their stadium events, which revealed that over **50%** of the men in attendance - were involved with pornography within **one week** of attending the event. *(Promise Keepers - large men's ministry in the U.S. with the slogan "Men of Integrity!")*

- 51% of pastors say cyber-porn is a possible temptation. 37% say it is a current struggle *(Christianity Today, Leadership Survey, 12/2001).*
- **Over half of evangelical pastors admit viewing pornography last year.**
- Roger Charman of Focus on the Family's Pastoral Ministries reports that approximately 20 percent of the calls received on their Pastoral Care Line are for help with issues such as **pornography and compulsive sexual behaviour.**
- In a 2000 Christianity Today survey, 33% of clergy admitted to having visited a sexually explicit Web site. Of those who had visited a porn site, 53% had visited such sites "a few times" in the past year, and

18% visit sexually explicit sites between a couple of times a month and more than once a week.

- **29% of born again adults in the U.S. feel it is "morally acceptable" to view movies with explicit sexual behaviour (*The Barna Group*).**
- 57% of pastors say that addiction to pornography is the most sexually damaging issue to their congregation (*Christians and Sex Leadership Journal Survey, March 2005*).

We could go on and on with such statistics but already it's very evident that in general society's standards of morality are slipping to an all time low and by all indications will continue in a pattern of steady decline.

As Christians we are not exempt from such temptations, something that has been openly proven, time and again. Sadly even our "moral-compass" is slipping! **Every one of us is capable of being "vehemently-outraged" by the very things we're struggling with ourselves!** Only the spiritually strong will survive, those who live by *faith and not by sight!*

We live in a particular time in history, where life as we know it is being sexually "super-charged." This is something that is totally premeditated from the devil's point of view and something that we cannot treat casually - as scripture warns; *"If the righteous scarcely be saved, where shall the ungodly and the sinner appear?" (1 Peter 4:18)* Also James 1:27 says, *"...keep ...unspotted from the world"* and 1 Timothy 5:22 adds, *"...keep thyself pure."*

The temptation to give in to evil comes from us and only us. We have no one to blame but the leering, seducing flare-up of our own lust...

(James 1:14 MSG)

To the pure all things are pure, nevertheless we must relentlessly *pursue* purity and even militantly *keep* ourselves pure. Not out of religious piety but motivated from a true desire for genuine godliness. Even though the world around us no longer recognizes *purity* as a virtue or desirable quality to be acquired.

In fact today's world celebrates *perversity* instead and *restraint* is more of a taboo! It's genuinely backward. Such reality TV programs like **"Big Brother"** have helped to promote such thinking and force what's generally considered the *norm* to change. Now more than ever, it is so critical for us to stay *spiritually awake* and not fall sway to the same kind of *numbness* that afflicts the world around us. Occurring on such levels that nothing *shocks* anymore and sin no longer *offends* like it used to.

We are led instead to believe that people are more *offended* or *shocked* by such things as the Nativity *(Mary, Joseph and Baby Jesus);* or greetings like "Happy Christmas" *(rather than "Happy Holiday!")* A side issue perhaps but what nonsense! In most things today *normality* is being exchanged for *abnormality* and perhaps more distinctively, *morality for immorality!*

Statistics on Women
with Pornography Addiction

- 28% those admitting to sexual addiction are women *(internet-filter-review.com)*.
- 34% of female readers of Today's Christian Woman's online newsletter admitted to intentionally accessing Internet porn in a recent poll and 1 out of every 6 women, including Christians, struggles with an addiction to pornography *(Today's Christian Woman, Fall 2003)*.

Statistics on Pornography's Effect
on Families and Marriages

- 47% percent of families said pornography is a problem in their home *(Focus on the Family Poll, October 1, 2003)*.
- The Internet was a significant factor in 2 out of 3 divorces *(American Academy of Matrimonial Lawyers in 2003 - divorcewizards.com)*. "At a 2003 meeting of the American Academy of Matrimonial Lawyers, two thirds of the 350 divorce lawyers who attended said the Internet played a significant role in the divorces in the past year, with excessive interest in online porn contributing to more than half such cases. Pornography had an almost non-existent role in divorce just seven or eight years ago." http://www.divorcewizards.com

Statistics on Child Pornography Use

- 9 out of 10 children aged between the ages of 8 and 16 have viewed pornography on the Internet, in most cases unintentionally *(London School of Economics January 2002)*.

- Average age of first Internet exposure to pornography: 11 years old. http://www.internet-filter-review.toptenreviews.com
- Largest consumer of Internet pornography: 12 - 17 year-old age group *(various sources, as of 2007)*.
- Adult industry says traffic is 20-30% children *(NRC Report 2002, 3.3)*.
- Youth with significant exposure to sexuality in the media were shown to be significantly more likely to have had intercourse at ages 14 to 16 *(Report in Paediatrics, April, 2006)*.

"Never before in the history of telecommunications media in the United States has so much indecent *(and obscene)* material been so easily accessible by so many minors in so many American homes with so few restrictions" - U.S. Department of Justice, Post Hearing Memorandum of Points and Authorities, at l, ACLU v. Reno, 929 F. Supp. 824 *(1996)*.

Statistics on Online Perpetrators

- 1 in 7 children who use the Internet have been sexually solicited - 2005. http://www.internet-filter-review.toptenreviews.com
- 1 in 4 kids participate in Real Time Chat. *(Family PC Survey, 2000)*.
- 1 in 5 children *(10 to 17 years old)* receives unwanted sexual solicitations online *(Youth Internet Safety Survey, U.S. Department of Justice, 2001)*.
- 2 in 5 abductions of children ages 15-17 are due to Internet contact *(San Diego Police Dept.)*

- 76% of victims in Net-initiated sexual exploitation cases were 13-15, 75% were girls. "Most cases progressed to sexual encounters" - 93% of the face-to-face meetings involved illegal sex *(Journal of Adolescent Health, November 2004,* http://www.unh.edu/ccrc/pdf/CV71.pdf).

❖

CHAPTER 7

Abnormal Sexual Behaviour

Sexual seduction is part of the fallen nature and therefore affects humanity as a whole, not just one people group. So *sexuality* can be generalised without singling out one specific group or another; in other words ALL SEXUALITY IS SUBJECT TO THE FALLEN NATURE AND IS BECOMING MORE & MORE PERVERSE regardless of specific orientations, *(we can not just single out the homosexuals because they are just one group out of many)*.

> *Refusing to know God, they soon didn't know how to be human either - women didn't know how to be women; men didn't know how to be men. Sexually confused, they abused and defiled one another, women with women, men with men, all lust, no love.*
>
> *(Romans 1:26-27 MSG)*

Nevertheless one of the changes that we are facing today as a worldwide community is the accommodation that is being made for the homosexual agenda. Whether it's same sex marriages, TV, changes in the law or so forth; homosexuality has become more and more *centre stage*, both in politics and in business.

Later we discuss what's considered to be the *pink-pound*, because whatever affects the economy, affects all of us! And all politicians and businesses want to embrace whatever affects their voting capacity or economic potential! Regardless of any differences in social standing, homosexuality is having an increasing influence on all of our lives, one way or another.

Subsequently it is crucial that we as believers do not mishandle this fact. The upsurge of perversity is affecting all walks of life, and there are a myriad of ways that people are choosing to express their sexuality today.

The media loves to indulge in the clash of interests between camps, making a - *them and us situation* - between gays and Christians. Many Christians have lacked wisdom and unfortunately gotten *embroiled* in the fight, forgetting that we are not up against flesh and blood. When we do not operate in love, we malign the gospel more than propel it *(Ephesians 6:12; John 13:35).*

Yes of course there is a fine line between this and compromise but I have to repeat it again and again that perversion exists in ALL PEOPLE GROUPS and you are never going to change that. Heterosexuals can be just as perverse as anyone else. That is a FACT!

However, for my wife and myself, it is our personal opinion that the worst forms of sexual perversion, are those committed against the *free will* of innocent children. But even then the bible does not distinguish between sins. Sin is sin; there are no big or small sins.

Perversion is perversion and we have all been guilty of it one way or another and at one time or another, on one level or another. We all needed saving from the *human condition* and we all needed a saviour and His name is still Jesus!

PERVERSION is a hard word to swallow and all gays alike hate to be considered dirty, perverse or diseased by anyone, especially not Christians. They have as many *human rights* as anyone else and with changes in the law to protect them more and more, it is simply not considered *politically correct* any more to single groups out or have prejudice issues of any kind.

My wife and I do not favour the disposition that attacks homosexuals. This is contrary to our faith. Jesus is the same Jesus who sat with the pimps, prostitutes and outcasts of His day. But the lines do get blurred and the bible must remain our incorruptible yardstick. It is the incorruptible seed. The living Word of God and every society that has ever been built upon its values and truths - has prospered and thrived. History is proof to this fact.

Current thinking that excludes Biblical values will back fire of course, because societies that uphold the premise that *anything goes (no restraint)* will eventually collapse. But in this world that we live in today, *freedom of speech* including *religious freedom* is gradually diminishing thanks to political correctness!

Therefore even though this particular chapter is taking a look at the nature of *homosexuality* specifically I can only continue to stress emphatically that other *orientations* are included and will be covered under the banner of "SEXUALITY" because it is all one and the same subject.

In my attempt to reach equilibrium *(balance)* I recommend you finish reading the whole book before drawing any premature conclusions. **Then I am confident that you will have no reason to take offence!**

So having drawn a curtain on the last chapters that looked solely at seduction of women *(especially in these end times)* we continue now with this topic of *homo*-sexuality, because it affects both genders; men and women. HOMO basically means "SAME" and is how we arrive at "Same-Sex Marriages" for example.

In these last days sex and sexuality overall is being hugely advanced; in other words, *accelerated* and *exaggerated* more than ever before. Yet this is a fluid concept *(without strict definition)* because having studied some of the pagan elements of the Roman Empire it's hard to believe that things could digress beyond that point again. Simply because some of the practices of the pagan world were so appallingly lewd and base that it's hard to fathom people going back to that again by volition, yet they *are* and they *will*.

In the Pagan world for instance, "orgies" and "sex-fests" were commonplace. Actually things got so bad *(it was so much the norm to practice homo-sex or have sex with animals, children or other)* that paganism's aristocracy actually scoffed at *heterosexuality* - consider that!

Nevertheless perversion of every kind is on the rise, so let's consider some FACTS. If you were to ask any psychologist today, to give a brief definition of *perversion,* their standard reply would be: "any *abnormal* means of obtaining sexual satisfaction."

In addition to this, any basic dictionary would define perversion as such:

- The act of perverting or the state of being perverted.
- A perverted form or usage.
- A curve that reverses the direction of something.
- The action of perverting something *(turning it to a wrong use); (i.e. "it was a perversion of justice")*
- Activity that transgresses moral or civil law.

To interject here; OFFENCE is such a BIG word these days I guess it's possible to gain *offence* even from a dictionary! But I have yet to hear of a lawsuit that's been taken out against a dictionary! Still altering our language to accommodate the changes in our common behaviour, is no doubt taking place *(simply because political correctness demands it from us!)*

To take this a step further, the word *sodomy* is still in the dictionary *(it is still also in the bible!)* The meaning of sodomy to several sources is as follows:

- Sexual intercourse involving anal or oral copulation
- Bestiality http://dictionary.reference.com/browse/sodomy
- Any of various forms of sexual intercourse held to be unnatural or abnormal, especially anal intercourse or bestiality http://www.thefreedictionary.com/sodomy

If you are not too *delicately* minded you might be willing to see how the urban dictionary defines sodomy, with it's own particular *vernacular* and *terminology!* Go online to urbandictionary.com and keep it real. Or use the following link: http://www.urbandictionary.com/define.php?term=sodomy

A very common and popular source of information today is **Wikipedia.** So I have included what Wiki has to say about Sodomy from its opening explanation: "Sodomy refers to anal sex or other non-penile/vaginal copulation-like acts, **especially between male persons or between a person and an animal.** [1] The word is derived from the story of Sodom and Gomorrah in chapters 18 and 19 of the *Book of Genesis* in the bible. [1] So-called 'sodomy laws' in many countries criminalized not only these behaviors, but other disfavored sexual activities as well, **but in the Western world, many of these laws have been overturned, or are not routinely enforced."** http://en.wikipedia.org/wiki/Sodomy

Going back to the word *perversion* from the previous page above, it is easy to see that the English language is clear when defining what is considered *perverse.* Yet one dictionary I found online gave a more rigorous definition for perversion that actually *included* sodomy. I quote, **"An aberrant sexual practice; sexual perversion - paraphilia - abnormal sexual**

activity: anal intercourse, anal sex, buggery, sodomy *(intercourse via the anus, committed by a man with a man or woman)."* http://www.thefreedictionary.com/perversion

So with this context of perversion at the forefront - as stipulated by the English language and not my personal opinion - in essence **perversion is taking something that is going in one direction and making it go in another - for which it was not fashioned or formed.** And this is where homosexuality comes into the plot.

For instance it would be correct to say that *procreation, reproduction, breeding and populating* - are all amongst the chief reasons for sex - regardless of relational value and the possibility for meaningful pleasure derived from such. Pleasure then is not the *only* purpose of sex rather an *additional benefit* or *bonus* of having sex! This is without mentioning anything about birth control and every other aspect about sex.

On face value alone - sex is vital to world population - something that would be literally *impossible* if everyone were *homo* or *same*-sexual. So by all intents and purposes sex is vital to the human race and does not just feature along the lines of pleasure or pain.

Let's be clear about this scientifically speaking. Anything *homo* - is completely *sterile* simply because it cannot *reproduce* itself like God *instructed* Adam and Eve in the garden, *"...be fruitful, multiply and replenish the earth" (Genesis 1:28).* God created Adam and Eve, not Adam and Steve, which would have been counterproductive and barren.

Now I understand that for gay couples this can be hurtful and a bitter pill to swallow. Also I am aware that each persons definition of *normal* differs greatly - therefore this is no longer a discussion of what is *normal* or *abnormal* rather what is *perverse* or not. In reality most languages have a clear definition for the word "perversion" much the same as our own *(English)* yet most folks would never like to think of themselves or be defined in such a way!

To add a little humour here and to stay in good standing with science, it's true to say that literally *anything* can become perverted. Even a plant that grows in the wrong direction! *(Yes you read correctly!)* Read this excerpt: **"Perversion is a curve that reverses the direction of something; i.e. the tendrils of the plant exhibited perversion... perversion also shows up in kinky telephone cords!"** http://www.thefreedictionary.com/perversion

However what was considered *perverse* in yesteryear is not necessarily considered perverse still today. Homosexuality has become more and more *acceptable.* A "conditioning" has occurred, largely due to the media, so that homosexuality is no longer considered *offensive* or even *sinful.* From politicians, to musicians and popular celebrities, homosexuality is *defended* so rigorously that everyone else who might think otherwise is branded **"homo-phobic."** *(However it is also possible today to be "hetero-phobic!")*

In fact the Gay Pride Movement has elevated its *agenda, course* and *social voice* so dramatically, that few are willing, any longer to stand against it. And while the masses conform to this radically changing world-view - Christians on the other hand have remained loyal to the biblical world-view.

This has entrenched them largely on the opposite side of the table, which outrages the gay movement. Who don't accredit Christians for their loyalty to their fundamentalist beliefs or faith, but instead see it as an overt and deliberate *attack* on their movement.

YET SCRIPTURE REMAINS! Even when public opinion changes and "political-will" morphs - God's Word remains the same!

According to the bible, homosexuality is a clear *perversion* of what God intended for His creation and is a bending of the natural curve. Regardless of faith or even the bible, the fact remains that if all the animals rebelled today and went *homo* then every single species on earth would eventually become extinct! Just as with the law of gravity, there is no human philosophy that could ever change that!

None of this is meant to *offend* anyone - after all when we put theology, philosophy and all other differences aside and just talk biology (*not prejudice, discrimination, hatred or narrow-mindedness*) the science can speak for itself!

I don't even think for a moment that even with the changes in worldview that all of a sudden everyone wants to become homosexual. They don't. **It is more an argument of acceptance versus tolerance.** Humanistically the arguments sound just and fair. **But what about the case of the bi-sexual who is not homosexual yet is strongly encouraged to abandon the side of himself that still desires a woman, in order to "come-out" and be considered gay.**

There are many shades of grey, but not of gay seemingly. Those who are bi-sexual are automatically seen as homosexual when they are not. People are often confused by the *"born-this-way"* argument that's been taken up onto centre stage even more with the help of such artists like Lady Gaga and others.

Yet when I was growing up I remember being told that around the age of 13 each person experiences a surge in their sexuality. This acts like a vital crossroads that can take a person one way or the other - depending on the influences surrounding them at that point, *(such as abuse or early exposure to sexual experiences).*

Still I'll keep emphasising it for what it really is, that at whatever age an individual gets in touch with their *sexuality (late or early bloomer)* it is all the same thing. Whether *bi, metro, hetro, homo or other…* it's all the same subject, just plain old fallen **SEXUAL-ITY.**

Satan understands that if he can confuse people at that crucial stage in life, then he can convince them one way or another, to step under a banner and be identified as such, while denying natural desires that are still present.

Either way, once again and very significantly the New Testament teaches us in Ephesians 6:12 that we are **not** up against flesh and blood but "principalities, against powers, against the rulers of the darkness of this world, against spiritual wickedness in high places." This is a *spiritual battle* and not something that we can hold against individuals for the violation of creation and its natural "ordained order."

Furthermore people can *and always will* - emotionally, physically and spiritually violate themselves if they so choose to do so but it's not God's *best* for them. Instead His *best* for them is life, not disease, sterility or even death *(see Deuteronomy 30:19).*

Now when one talks about sin, I am one who agrees with the argument that says gluttony is just as much a sin as any other. If we were to speak about **obesity** then that would surly cause some major offence for the overweight crowd! Nevertheless it is intriguing how much we tend to *segregate* sin into neat labelled boxes - making some sins seem so *great* while others are much more *tolerable!*

However scripture is faultless in saying that, **"everyone has sinned; we all fall short of God's glorious standard"** *(Romans 3:22-24 NLT).* I know that writing about this subject of homosexuality will not change the facts - nevertheless some folks in Christendom have very little understanding about these issues and have even become intimidated or frightened to speak out - in case they are deemed *politically incorrect* or might infringe someone else's basic *human rights.* **Oh how we *hate* to *offend* in this 21st century!**

Yet scripture clearly states, *"We preach Christ crucified... a stumbling block ...foolishness. But God hath chosen the foolish things of the world to confound the wise" (1 Corinthians 1:19-28).* In verse 19 it says, *"Where is the* DISPUTER *of this world?"* Also meaning the SOPHIST of this world. It is true, we become so SOPHIST-*ICATED* and humanistic that we miss the simplicity of the scriptures and its life saving, life changing meaning *(Romans 1:16).*

Now as we have stated before, it is within a person's right to be gay if they so choose. Others say they have no choice because they were "born this way." Others say that they were abused at an early age which helped influence their orientation. Others still, say they were confused about their sexuality and found their sexual identity as a result of "sexual-experimentation."

Psychologists who study the science of "human-behaviour" site many reasons for homosexuality but it simply comes down to the "fallen nature" of man, which is something that their *behavioural-science* cannot explain away!

❖

CHAPTER 8

Extreme Self Indulgence

I n this chapter we will continue right where we left off concerning homosexuality and all other forms of sexual vice including incest and bestiality. So as we delve deeper, let us begin with a handful of scriptures that deal directly with this very subject. For instance in Daniel 11:37, many people believe that Daniel spoke about the "antichrist" as being a homo-sexual, *"Neither shall he regard the God of his fathers, nor **the desire of women...**"*

> *Don't have sex with a man as one does with a woman. That is abhorrent.*
>
> *(Leviticus 18:22 MSG)*

Then in the Authorized Version of the bible, Deuteronomy 23:18 says, *"Thou shalt not bring the hire of a whore, or **the price of a dog,** into the house of the LORD thy God for any vow: for even* *both these are abomination unto the LORD thy God."* What many people wouldn't know is that the word used here for **"dog"** in this particular scripture was used in the original Hebrew as a euphemism for **"male prostitute"** *(Strong's Hebrew #3611).* In fact during the Old Testament many "temple-prostitutes" existed - both male and female.

The Message Bible actually uses the words **"sacred-prostitute"** and **"priest-pimp"** instead! *"No daughter of Israel is to become a **sacred prostitute**; and no son of Israel is to become a **sacred prostitute.** And don't bring the fee of a **sacred whore or the earnings of a priest-pimp** to the house of GOD, your God, to pay for any vow - they are both an abomination to GOD, your God"* (Deuteronomy 23:18; also see 1 Kings 14:24).

It is also true that during the Old Testament there was very little tolerance towards homosexuality as seen here in Leviticus 20:13, *"If a man lies with a male as if he were a woman, both men have committed an offense (something perverse, unnatural, abhorrent, and detestable); they shall surely be put to death; their blood shall be upon them"* (AMP).

In Leviticus chapter 18 it talks about all manner of sexual vice, from incest, rape, human sacrifice to even **"bestiality"** *(sex with animals)* verse 23 says, *"Neither shall you lie with any beast and defile yourself with it; neither shall any woman yield herself to a beast to lie with it; it is confusion, perversion, and degradedly carnal"* (AMP).

The bible is clearly not shocked by such behaviour as seen today; Ecclesiastes 1:9 says, *"History merely repeats itself. It has all been done before. Nothing under the sun is truly new"* (NLT).

According to the late Derek Prince the city of Sodom was totally "given over" to a brazen, aggressive & violent form of homosexuality. As a respected bible teacher, I would like to bring out some of his remarks here concerning Genesis 19:5 where this aggressive form of homosexual behaviour was taking place.

"They called to Lot, Where are the men who came to you tonight? **Bring them out to us so that we can have sex with them"** *(NIV).* Now Derek Prince in his book titled: "Prophetic Guide to the End Times - Facing the Future without Fear" expounds this text very well by saying the following:

"The name of the city 'Sodom' in the English language was applied to a particular form of sexual perversion called 'sodomy,' now misnamed as 'being gay.'" Of the type of homosexuality displayed in Genesis chapter 19 Derek Prince wrote,

"This particular version of homosexuality was brazen; it came right out in the open. It made no pretence and offered no concealment. It was not passive; it was aggressive. It went out looking for its victims, searched for them with determination and was prepared to resort to physical violence... it embraced both young and old... **'all the men from the city** - both young and old.' This city's male population was apparently **totally given over to this brazen, aggressive, violent form of homosexuality...** and it ignored accepted standards of behaviour."

Concerning the *real* sin of Sodom he goes on to say, "I want to add one important note. **Many people think the real sin of Sodom was homosexuality, but that is not what**

God charges it with... Ezekiel 16:49 addressed to the city of Jerusalem, compares Jerusalem with Sodom, and this is what the Lord says about Sodom: 'Look, this was the iniquity of our sister Sodom: she and her daughter [that is, her fellow cities] had pride, fullness of food, and abundance of idleness; neither did she strengthen the hand of the poor and needy.'

There is no mention of homosexuality. I am not saying that God is indifferent toward homosexuality, far from it. But the basic sins of Sodom were SELFISHNESS, CARNALITY, SELF-INDULGENCE, LOOKING AFTER NUMBER ONE."

Derek Prince concludes by saying, "This is just my opinion, but I believe the Sodom kind of culture will always produce homosexuality. That is why we have so many homosexuals in the world today - because the sins of our day are just like the sins of Sodom: **'Pride, fullness of food, and abundance of idleness, neither did she strengthen the hand of the poor and needy.'**

How well does that describe our contemporary culture? We can lament the upsurge of homosexuality, but I believe the Sodom type of culture as described in Ezekiel 16 will always produce homosexuality. **HOMOSEXUALITY IS NOT THE ROOT. THE ROOT IS SELFISHNESS, SELF-INDULGENCE AND INDIFFERENCE TO OTHERS"** *(Prophetic Guide to the End Times, p91-93).*

This is revealed in our society in many ways but let's take a brief look at **"The Burning Man."** Homosexuality is not new and as we have seen, has been around since the time of Noah and Lot - well before Jesus walked the earth and it has always been controversial!

I introduce you to this annual event called, **"The Burning Man"** for the sake of keeping this *contemporary* and to help illustrate the points being made in this chapter.

Much more intense than other festivals of its kind like Glastonbury and others, the BM is many times more lewd. There is none like this event. With its major hatred towards God, extreme self expression, neo-paganism, orgies, sex rituals, new age philosophy, deep humanism, idolatry, occultism, satanic symbolism and the practice of witchcraft, sexual vice on every level *(including homosexuality and paedophilia)* with an overall rebellion and hatred for anything authority. Again I introduce, **"The Burning Man."**

The founders of which vehemently oppose the suggestion that it is religious in any way; yet every type of worship occurs there including ancient Egyptian rituals - all except Christianity.

This event takes place each year in the middle of nowhere. Hidden in the desert miles from anywhere, in **Nevada Black Rock Desert** - where 50,000 *plus* gather each year to build a pseudo/temporary city - for one week during the "Summer Solstice" *(a witchcraft holiday)* and whose population explodes each year to house every type of rebellion against God imaginable - **in one place, at one time.** *(See* http://www. burningman.com*)*.

Some years ago, in 2001 a particular Christian named James Whistler went to "The Burning Man" in order to report back what he saw there. *(To read his article in full, called "Satan's Birthday Party" visit the link provide below)*. Within his eye-opening article James shows a photograph of one of the "huge" pieces of artwork *(with homosexual theme)* at the festival - sporting a slogan that read, **"No more censorship!! Ban homophobia!!"** and **"We're not going back into the closet!!"** Other artwork unashamedly celebrated sodomy and paedophilia behaviour. One piece of artwork in particular, which was life-sized, showed an image of Jesus engaged in the act of sodomy with a young boy!

Within the article he said, "My heart went out to one little boy about 5 or 6 years old who was being paraded around in the nude with his spiked fluorescent hairdo, by his fully-clothed mother. I could just imagine the number of pedophiles drooling over that poor child. I was ever so thankful to the Lord that I didn't see very many children there. One theme camp took it upon themselves to provide a giant projection screen TV with pornographic movies for the crowds or passers-by."

"Certainly everyone there, in one-way or another, was trying to reflect or communicate their beliefs. This includes as many pagan and occultist persuasions as you can imagine." http://poweredbychrist.homestead.com/BurningMan.html

Make your own study of such events. But you will be shocked at the level of paganism and occultism involved, going on *blatantly* with the general public remaining unaware!

Now I want to add this important consideration. It is currently within the rights of any individual to *express* their sexuality via as many avenues as they see fit; *same-sex-relations* are just one of them. But being gay is one of the more accepted expressions today and increasingly considered as *normal*. This clearly differentiates on the definition of normal from just decades ago.

If what is considered *normal* today was still highly offensive just decades ago - then where will this definition of *normal* eventually stretch *(and how fast?)* What if for instance, one individual considers it within their right to have *multiple partners (adultery)* while another considers it within their rights to have sex with animals? Who decides and at what rate do these patterns of what is considered acceptable or not shift?

Sadly and evidently some people today feel it within their right to express their sexuality by having sex with children, using such arguments as: "I was born this way. This is the way that I am. It is *normal* for me..." Should then this type of behaviour automatically become acceptable or even normal over time? I would certainly hope not. ***But alas it is already happening!***

To prove this point I will briefly introduce to you the existence of **a political party in the Netherlands that promotes paedophilia.** *(Yes really!)* It's hard to believe and this group did manage to stir up much debate and controversy while they lasted. But the fact remains that they still existed and felt it within their rights to openly express their beliefs without any shame whatsoever. Even tried bending the curve of *normality* in their favour and to their own advantage!

Again I say that it's hard to believe, but I quote the article as follows: "Pedophiles in the Netherlands are registering a political party to press for lowering the legal age of sexual relations from 16 to 12 and allow child porn and bestiality. On its website, the Charity, *Freedom and Diversity Party* declares: 'We are going to shake The Hague awake!'"

Thankfully the same article later goes onto say: "Although the Netherlands already has liberal policies permitting prostitution and same-sex marriage, opinion polls show the public isn't *ready* for a pedophile party. In a survey published today, 67 percent believe promoting pedophilia should be illegal, and 82 percent want the government to do something to stop the party's formation." *(You can find this article at:* http://www.wnd.com/2006/05/36408.*)*

That political party did disband just years later after failing to have any success. Nevertheless, if the general public of the Netherlands were not *"ready* for a pedophile party" at the time of that particular opinion poll, does that suggest they will be ready or more sympathetic in the future? If this is the case, then it's just a matter of time.

I'd like to add, that this is exactly where so called "liberality" leads: false liberty, bondage, social decay and decadence.

So in a world that no longer looks to the bible for answers and where there is little restraint or accountability - who now decides what levels of decency and acceptability to go by? What levels of self-expression will be indulged before violation occurs? Especially considering those who see that sex with children is not wrong - as long as there is *consent.* But who decides if there is genuine consent or not, when children are rarely articulate and aren't aware of their rights? *(Children only go where they are **taken**).*

It's utterly incredible to think that a real debate even exists today, concerning "consensual-sex" between adults and children *(mutual consent in such cases is not possible, unless severe **conditioning** is involved).* It's truly bizarre to imagine and even more so that a group of people would actually deem it necessary to raise a political voice in *The Hague* to speak on behalf of or in favour of such diabolical nonsense!

Even though laws do protect children today - it is only to a point. Such laws are also subject to change and are feeble in the sight of human traffickers, who unlawfully trample underfoot the rights of children, every time they put children on sale like merchandise or a lucrative commodity.

Evidently without the bible there are no authentic *guidelines* to live by. People have become a *law-unto-themselves* and everything has become a *free-for-all,* not just in the sex arena but also in everything and there is always huge potential for abuse when everyone is *taking (to fulfil their own pleasures) rather* than *giving.* Conversely when everyone is *giving* like scripture teaches, then everyone receives. After all, the guidelines laid down throughout scripture are there for our *protection* not *abuse.*

It should have become evident to you by now, that there is much more to this than narrow minded arguments such as, "let's fight the homosexual agenda or judge everyone who is not like us" *(particularly from a Church point of view).*

Nevertheless I have attempted in this book to address this volatile subject matter in the context of its entirety, it is NOT just a "homosexual" issue. In fact it is not even just a SEXUAL issue but one much deeper than that. As Derek Prince rightly pointed out; homosexuality is not just a *sexual* sin; it has much deeper roots behind it and is largely *symptomatic* of the real causes.

If therefore anyone wanted to make a target-study of *homosexuality* and the *homosexual-spirit* then they would also be well advised to study *adultery* and the *spirit of adultery!* In essence it is all the same thing, just different variations on the expression of sin and the fallen nature. Personally I am very wary of isolating one set of sins above others. This is very dangerous. However this does not make me pro-gay nor am I a liberal, but I *can* see that there are much wider issues at hand *(see Derek Prince's quote on p73-74 of this book)*.

So why include adultery in this? Obviously because it involves sexual vice, in fact today it is estimated that 50% of pastors marriages will end in divorce, a truly shocking statistic. What's equally as disturbing is that some high profile ministers are so publically divorced one day and back in the pulpit and on international TV the next. *With a business as usual profile!* However the realities of divorce are just not that simple. The repercussions are far too great. It takes years for full *restoration* to take place, especially where children and congregations are involved.

Judgment starts in the house of God, especially within the leadership of the Church. So we have much to *target* ourselves with were sin is concerned. Sadly sin is as much rampant in the Church as in the world - certainly in some cases!

Truth is, wherever there are people present, there is always sin present! So when leaders must deal with the sins of the people, it must be done with *much* humility, as evidently *none* of us are immune! *"If a man be overtaken in a fault, ye which are spiritual, restore such a one **in the spirit of meekness; considering thyself, lest thou also be tempted"** (Galatians 6:1).*

❖

CHAPTER 9

Sodomy Today

A s we continue to navigate our way through this subject, it's evident that many Christians fear *reprisal* if they speak out. However it depends how you speak out. Being verbal just for the sake of being verbal *(or opinionated)* is not smart and entering the debate just to appear *relevant* is not enough.

"There is a Tolerance for Everything BUT Christianity!"
(Gianna Jessen - Abortion Survivor <u>www.giannajessen.com</u>*)*

On the other hand if we remain *mute* on such weighty topics, **we end up relinquishing our own rights!** So it's in our best interest and those of our children, to stand up for what we believe in *(everyone else does!)* We just better be *sure* of what we believe before *verbalising* too much, as weighty subjects do bear weighty responsibility, *(when you dare to* *address them)*. The alternatives are NOT an option; silence is not always virtue as Plato says below:

> *"The price of apathy towards public affairs is to be ruled by evil men" (Plato - Ancient Greek Philosopher).*

What we are engaged in goes beyond mere *soapboxing* and *vocalizing* our religious opinions or airing our individual views. There is much more to this; we are engaged in a spiritual battle, whether we like it or not. And our words are *cheap* unless they are words of faith! Besides, as bible believing Christians we are *accountable* for our beliefs before the Lord; we are not just facing a world stage, we are facing God Himself!

In particular any preacher who is *not* declaring truth, will have to answer for that before the Lord! We must project beliefs that hold genuine *conviction* behind them, **not just mental and intelligent arguments!** Gone are the days where mere religious-behaviour is enough. There must be weight behind our faith - especially when *tested!* And tested we will be, as the Message Bible says so articulately;

> *I know how great this makes you feel, even though you have to put up with every kind of aggravation in the meantime. Pure gold put in the fire comes out of it proved pure;* **genuine faith put through this suffering comes out proved genuine.** *When Jesus wraps this all up,* **it's your faith, not your gold, that God will have on display as evidence of his victory.**

> *(1 Peter 1:7)*

We are going to have to make a choice in these times; to speak our faith with conviction and wisdom so that others can be equipped and instructed or to be *muted* and *censured* by political correctness, where the truth is left untold. Will we choose to hide *incognito* like some *secret society* or *elite-religious-order (via fear)* or be open and transparent *(via faith)?* A time is coming where Christians will have to go *under-ground* but until that time fully arrives, we owe it to the rest of the world to proclaim God's truth fearlessly and full of faith!

Also let's remember that Paul wrote large portions of the New Testament, whilst stuck in prison or house arrest! Nothing could stop him and we need the same ethic! Even minority groups such as those protesting for "gay rights," have only grown *(in such phenomenal strength)* today because in the face of *opposition* they did not run and hide, but have relentlessly "spoken-out" about their rights.

So what about the rights of the believer? Are we going to enforce our agenda too, regardless of the opposition or are we much too idle and apathetic, that we allow our rights to be whittled away? Will we wait until it's too late?

Opting for the safe posture of "self-preservation" by saving ourselves from the conflict - does not make the conflict automatically go away! Rather it will gain in strength while we sleep. Perhaps we should adhere to the military term that says, "The best defence is offence," which is NOT a passive sentiment!

Throughout history, whenever they tried to "clamp" the gospel it spread more vehemently instead. Though persecution has never actually died-out! It has always been rife within the world and Christianity that declares the name of Jesus has never been *(or ever will be)* politically *correct* within the public domain.

Paul himself was politically *incorrect* and did not try and fit in with the political culture of his day. Yet look how God used him and how God will use us! What would Paul say about the events of our world today? Would he allow himself to be muted and silenced so easily? No sir! And neither should we allow fear to dictate our beliefs. Silent faith has no affect on anyone, because faith without works *(or even words)* is dead! *(James 2:20)* **Silent faith is a false kind of faith that masquerades as faith, but is action-less and voice-less!**

However it is significant at this point to understand that our warfare is spiritual. Repeatedly I will draw attention to the fact that we are never up against people. Ephesians 6:12 states that we are not fighting "flesh and blood."

No! Our warfare is totally spiritual and spirits of *lust* are influencing and actively *degrading* our societies; we cannot idly sit and passively watch without objection. What is our faith good for if we are no longer *salty* to the world around us - has our salt so easily lost its flavour? *(Matthew 5:13)*

According to scripture, lust is something that *burns* within us *(1 Corinthians 7:9 and Isaiah 57:5)* and something that we must guard against. The following scripture pulls no punches at all!

Don't be naive. There are difficult times ahead. As the end approaches, people are going to be self-absorbed...

profane... ADDICTED TO LUST, and allergic to God. They'll make a show of religion, but behind the scenes they're animals.

(2 Timothy 3:4 MSG)

In a world of "no-restraint" bible-believing Christians are considered *fundamentalists* or even *extremists* and are very unpopular with the sort of crowd who want to dabble in every kind of *sexual-expressionism* there is. It is certain that we are no longer politically correct just as Gianna Jessen said recently, whom I have quoted in our opening statement. *(By the way I strongly recommend that you watch her powerful testimony on YouTube via the link given here below, including her website called bornalivetruth.org It will be an eye opener!)* http://youtu.be/kPF1FhCMPuQ

However our unpopularity exists for many reasons *(some self inflicted, especially when believers lack wisdom)* but primarily because of the scriptures that we confess and believe. They are stumbling block and threaten the freedoms, belief systems and philosophies of the world and their way of life.

Once again what are the alternatives? Do we succumb to the pressure to alter scripture, as we know it, just to accommodate modern thinking? Or even OMIT such scriptures that cause the most offense? Certainly not! This would alter the very fabric of our faith. What other religion would accept such conditions? The answer is "None."

Besides once we start doing that, where would it end - until the whole bible is dismantled? The answer must be that, scripture *offends* because it is *meant* to. According to Jesus, His Word brings *separation (Matthew 10:33-36; Revelations 22:18).*

However even with all political, philosophical, ethical, moral and psychological debates aside - it is not rocket science to be able to recognise that human *genitalia (as God fashioned it)* perfectly accommodates the opposite sex. In other words, a *vagina* was perfectly proportioned to receive the *(penetration of a) penis* and vice versa. Alternatively it's just as easy to recognise that an *anus* was perfectly fashioned to expel toxins and waste, *(the ONLY function intended for it!)*

Sodomy *(anal sex)* is a perversion of natural order. Again I say that when we pervert *the natural order of gravity* we pay a hefty price. The same is true of *the natural order of sex*. As mentioned in previous chapters, God generously designed sexual intercourse to be pleasurable NOT painful *(such as child birth)*. Only through *perversion* is pain derived from sex, instead of the true pleasure that God intended for it. In fact if we go about it, *any other way than what God intended, we outdo ourselves!*

So when it comes to the definition of "perversity" it's no good being aggressively *upset* with the bible *(or Christians who sincerely believe it verbatim)*, because it's a language issue. Any dictionary in the world can give a precise definition of *perversion (in any language)*. Perversion is perversion - you can't put a politically correct or positive spin on it! It is what it is, regardless of what the bible says or what people believe.

Consequently regardless of definitions or word-games, when an individual chooses to live a lifestyle that involves regular acts of sodomy - this decision is theirs to make - but we will see very clearly below, sodomy is officially still an unlawful act, although is generally only enforced when sodomy is *forced* without consent.

Views on homosexuality have changed so dramatically that our society is much less damning than it used to be *(it's rare today to punish sodomy unless implicated in rape charges - even though anti-sodomy laws do exist).*

However, reflecting on the stark contrast of past generations, let's consider the likes of "Leonardo Da Vinci," who was strongly believed by many in his day, to be gay. In his early twenties Leonardo was arrested and accused of performing *sodomy* with a young male prostitute. Making him famous not only for his love of the arts but also for pretty young boys! *(He was penchant for the constant presence of young male models!)*

His society was far less tolerant than ours and he narrowly missed being *hung* for his crime, except for a last minute intervention by some powerful friends! However even with all the changes in spiritual-climate and political-will today, nothing can alter the bible! No matter how much anger it stirs up or evokes.

It is common knowledge that the act of sodomy and the lifestyle of homosexuality are synonymous. This makes it difficult to separate the person from the sin. But as believers we must tolerate the individual without taking on their beliefs systems. As I always say, we need wisdom in handling such issues and must always *love* people - WITHOUT compromising our beliefs.

In the past there was bullying and discrimination towards homosexuals *(which I do NOT condone).* Now however they are gaining ground and strength as a minority group.

But in a world where freedom of speech and human rights have actually stifled our rights and our freedoms - where do we go from here? The answer has to be "FAITH AND NOT FEAR!"

FACT: "anti-sodomy laws" are still in place today. When doing some research recently, I discovered some facts about "State Laws on Sex Crimes" in the USA and an article entitled: "When is Sodomy Unlawful?" It is interesting that with all the debate around the legalisation of *same sex marriage* and the continual upsurge of homosexuality - specific laws against sodomy are still very much intact throughout the US. Meaning that if there was the necessary *political-will* behind it, then it could still be enforced to penalize sodomy today if found guilty. On the books it is still referred to officially as, **"Crime Against Nature."** As follows:

"According to criminaldefenselawyer.com historically, the act of sodomy *(the Sin of Sodom)*, which is basically anal penetration, was held by courts as 'deviant' and was punished harshly. **In some cases, the law's language extended to acts of oral penetration and bestiality.**

Although most statutes did not expressly state the purposes of the law, it was impliedly known that these laws were basically laws against homosexual acts. In the U.S. during the 50s, every state had some variation of law criminalizing the act of sodomy. The pivotal 2003 case of *Lawrence v. Texas* nullified all state anti-sodomy laws that penalized consensual sex done in privacy. **However, a few dissenting states still retain anti-sodomy laws in their criminal codes and seek to enforce them.**

State Law

Since *Lawrence,* most states have repealed their sodomy laws. Only a few states retain anti-sodomy laws on their books, usually referred to as **'crimes against nature'** or **'deviate sexual intercourse.'** Among those dissenting states *(with penalties)* are:

• **Alabama** - 13A-6-65(a)(3). Sexual Misconduct. 'He or she engages in deviate sexual intercourse with another person.' Consent is no defence. Misdemeanour punishable by a fine up to $2,000 and/or up to 1 year imprisonment.

• **North Carolina** - 14-177. Crime Against Nature. Carnality 'with mankind or beast' *(no gender restriction).* Felony punishable up to 3 years imprisonment.

• **Oklahoma** - 21-886. Crime Against Nature. 'Committed with mankind and beast *(same sex only).'* Felony punishable up to 10 years imprisonment.

• **Texas** - 21.06. Homosexual Conduct. 'Deviate sexual intercourse with another individual of the same sex.' Misdemeanour. $500 fine.

• **Virginia** - 18.2-361. Crimes Against Nature. Both homosexual and heterosexual, anal and oral penetration. Includes bestiality. Felony punishable up to 5 years imprisonment." http://www.criminaldefenselawyer.com/ resources/criminal-defense/sex-crimes/when-sodomy-unlawful

Another easy source of information concerning official legalities still surrounding *sodomy* today - is the online

"Legal-Dictionary" *(accessible to anyone for research)*. Let me add a brief excerpt here, as follows:

"**Sodomy** n. anal copulation by a man inserting his penis in the anus either of another man or a woman. **If accomplished by force, <u>without consent</u>, or with someone incapable of consent, sodomy is a felony in all states in the same way that rape is.** Homosexual *(male to male)* sodomy between consenting adults has also been found a felony, but increasingly is either decriminalized or **seldom prosecuted.**

Sodomy with a consenting adult female is virtually never prosecuted even in those states in which it **remains on the books as a criminal offence.** However, there have been a few cases, including one in Indiana, in which a now-estranged wife insisted that a husband be charged with sodomy for sexual acts while they were living together. **Traditionally sodomy was called 'the crime against nature.'** Sodomy does not include oral copulation or sexual acts with animals *(bestiality) (See: rape, bestiality)*." http://legal-dictionary. thefreedictionary.com/sodomy

Crime against *nature* means that sodomy is still legally considered as an unlawful **"curve that reverses the direction of something,"** *(see definition No.3 of the word perversion on p63 of this book).*

Now I don't doubt for a moment that homosexual couples do genuinely experience meaningful unions, as much as heterosexual couples do. Some are even life-long *monogamous* relationships *(one partner)* and others are serial *polygamists (multiple partners simultaneously)* but this is something that any sexual *orientation* is capable of and still does not negate the bible.

Whether gay, bi or hetero - we are all capable of fidelity or infidelity. We are all capable of perversion no matter who we are. And we are not discussing personality here nor the human rights of gay individuals, but the much wider topic of "human-sexuality" and **Satan's all-out-agenda to pervert everyone of us - to divide and enrage us against one another.** He hates humanity. Perversion is his "prize weapon" that keeps us away from knowing God intimately as we were designed to, spiritually *(not sexually!)*

❖

CHAPTER 10

Preferred Orientation

We know there are many different sexual "orientations" nowadays but the most commonly known are; heterosexual, bisexual, and homosexual *(including lesbian)* however there is also a newer term that is not so familiar, which is called **"metro-sexual."**

> *God gave them over and abandoned them to vile affections and degrading passions. For their women exchanged their natural function for an unnatural and abnormal one, and the men also turned from natural relations with women and were set ablaze (burning out, consumed) with lust for one another...*
>
> *(Romans 1:26-27 AMP)*

According to the online "Urban Dictionary" this terminology is defined as, "...a normally straight male who possesses qualities of a gay male *without being attracted to men*. A metro often appreciates the finer things in life and enjoys making himself look good; be it through styling his hair or wearing fashionable clothes."

Apparently "metros" are often, "mistaken for being gay because of their fashion sense and hygiene habits...!" It goes onto say, "An American metro-sexual is like your average European male. In France or Italy, men can be manly and work on cars and know about art and fashion at the same time.

They are cool with that and don't need some special name for their less *masculine* side. In the U.S. we think men all have to be either dumb gorillas or homosexuals. There is some grey area!" www.urbandictionary.com

Interestingly most folks are blissfully unaware that such terminology exists! The metro-man is a new phenomenon for many.

Nevertheless whether - homo/bi/hetero or metro - it's all related to sexuality. We are *all* sexual beings and were created to be *sexual*. I will repeatedly reiterate that *every* orientation that exists is guilty of *perversion* not just homosexuality. Therefore we must never adopt a self-righteous posture - it never helps - and certainly won't help us effectively reach homosexuals for Christ!

Instead we must humbly but steadfastly present the truth *(without compromise or fear)* even though the truth has the potential to OFFEND, we must never forget that it has the power to LIBERATE!

We must never take the opportunity of *receiving or rejecting* the Gospel away from people. We must never try to protect or rescue folks from being *offended* by the truth. This is motivated only by self-preservation and fear, rather than a genuine passion for their salvation. *(Jesus had the opportunity to rescue himself from the cross but He didn't take it!)* Therefore truth must never be concealed or muzzled and we should never be *"...ashamed of the gospel of Christ: for it is the power of God unto* SALVATION*" (Romans 1:16).* Yes it offends BUT it also saves!

Consider those very people you are tempted to protect from being "offended" by the Gospel - might just believe it and be set free!

The precise reason I continually point out we are *all capable of perversion* is because of our own "fallen nature" *(our own human condition without God that we all experienced!)* None of us can be self-righteous. Everyone of us was born into sin! Now however we can overcome this world and the fallen nature, by being born of God instead *(1 John 5:1,4,18).* With this in mind **we must all avoid the self-righteous attitude of "finger-pointing."**

We all come into the Kingdom with an unregenerate mind; perhaps even with some demonic strongholds or oppressions. Plus sanctification - the process of putting off the old man and putting on the new - is an arduous one that we are all subject to. Not one of us hit-the-ground-running, in other words none of us are perfect, even when we became born again. But thankfully we have been given the opportunity through Christ to yield to His Spirit and start living our lives from the "inside-out" rather than vice versa - where the flesh used to dictate our every move!

We all have the opportunity to stubbornly follow our "earthy-animal-instincts" or surrender to the Holy Spirit and be convicted by His purity - where we can be forgiven, our minds renewed and our lives transformed *(see 1 John 1:9)*. It's always good to know that we can be forgiven, but also purified. We all needed to be "cleansed from unrighteousness" because it left its ugly stain on all of us, *(until we took up our precious robes of righteousness)*.

We must resist a *holier than thou, pious attitude*. In fact nowhere does religion give us the right to be "superior." Instead we better keep our own lives in check because nothing separates us from sin other than the cross of Jesus Christ. In other words **the only difference between the world and us is that we have accepted the work of the cross and they have not yet.** 1 John 1:9 stands for all of us who are still in the sanctification process; *"If we confess our sins, he is faithful and just and will forgive us our sins and **purify** us from all unrighteousness"* (NIV).

Today even many so-called "believers" no longer come to Christ for forgiveness because they don't see that they have sinned or done anything wrong. However whether we are sinner or saint, once again the Message Bible helps us out with its awesome clarity,

If we claim that we're free of sin, we're only fooling ourselves. A claim like that is errant nonsense. On the other hand, if we admit our sins - make a clean breast of

them - he won't let us down; he'll be true to himself. He'll forgive our sins and purge us of all wrongdoing. If we claim that we've never sinned, we out-and-out contradict God - make a liar out of him. A claim like that only shows off our ignorance of God.

(1 John 1:8-10 MSG)

To continue however it has to be said that the gay community vehemently resent being seen as "perverse" or "diseased!" To prove this point I quote again from the "urbandictionary.com" where its definition of a homosexual states;

"Homosexuality is not a perversion or a disease, but merely an aspect of sexuality that has been around for thousands of years..." (Note: take caution when you read this online dictionary, it's used here because it represents a general world-view).

It goes on to say, "Why are so many people homophobic? Homosexuals are great! Men should like gays... homosexuals by default don't add to the already grossly swollen human population." *(Note: this is an opinion held by many in the world today... who also strongly defame and vilify the bible for its stance on homosexuality - but I refrain from quoting such language!)*

Now I don't use any of this to *defend, advocate or promote* an argument FOR homosexuality as some ministers are doing right now. Other ministers go even further by deciding all of a sudden that they were gay all along! For instance recently I saw a minister in the USA who used an interview on TV as his "coming-out" opportunity. *(Sharing about it in such a manner that it sounded much like an overcoming testimony of struggles finally faced!)*

During the interview he admitted feeling *liberated* by his confessions that even after many years of happy marriage, with his wife and several children, he had really been gay all along! The interview showed many pictures of him with his children and grandchildren. All looked well. Yet his struggle went undetected for decades.

Now he is a strong advocate for the homosexual agenda. He took a 360 degree turn, even in what he teaches in his church and despite loosing most of his congregation, he continues with his new mandate! So as you can see the deceptions are real and so appealing. The stories sound so convincing that many people are altering their opinions.

Recently I read an article online about this very subject. The difference between the two, is the subject of great debate for some people, yet Asher a young *twenty-something* Jew from Denver, Colorado USA, simply wrote the following:

"In our day and age, the terms **'tolerance'** and **'acceptance'** have become interchangeable. This is a terrible development because it has led to different groups imposing their way of life on others under the guise of tolerance. Here is the basic difference that has been lost:

Tolerance - the capacity to disagree with someone or something, but put up with it anyway

Acceptance - the act of approving someone or something

While we must be able to tolerate those who differ with us, it doesn't mean we have to *accept* their opinions or way of life. The only exception to this is when it comes to basic ethical standards. For example, tolerating murder, theft, or physical abuse will lead to the moral dissolution of society.

However, we have to allow others the freedom to form their own views on the more subjective areas of life. Overall, tolerance is a virtue - and perhaps the most difficult to inculcate." http://levechad.blogspot.com/2010/06/difference-between-tolerance-and.html

So in essence *tolerance* is good and we must exercise such a sentiment. However it can also be used as clever propaganda in order to miss-lead and pressure people into *siding-with* sentiments that are not necessarily their own - to avoid being seen as *intolerant or hateful*.

Jesus was seemingly "silent" about this specific gay issue; does this mean He was tolerant? Some might see it that way. *(We have all tried to bend scripture to fit our circumstances at one time or other!)* The truth however is that Jesus was NOT silent at all - instead He spoke of "fornication" as being "sin," which covers the whole spectrum of our sexuality *(subject to the fallen nature)*. In Matthew 5:32 it says, *"...whosoever shall put away his wife, saving for the cause of **fornication**, causeth her to commit adultery..."*

The Greek word *porneia* used for fornication here means: idolatry, harlotry, adultery and incest as well as fornication *(see Strong's #4202)*. And fornication basically is; "premarital sex" or "any" willing sex outside of marriage - including extra-marital *(adultery)*.

According to the bible fornication is SIN. And this is what Jesus specifically had to say about SIN, *"I assure you, most solemnly I tell you, whoever commits and practices sin is the slave of sin"* (John 8:34 AMP). The rest of the bible has much to say about fornication, as seen in the following scriptures: Romans 6:12-14; 1 Corinthians 6:9-10; 13+18; 7:2; 10:6-8; 7:2; 2 Corinthians 10:3-5; Ephesians 5:1-3, 5; Galatians 5:19-21; 1 Thessalonians 4:3-5; Revelations 21:7-8.

According to John 1:1-4 below, Jesus is the Word of God and even though He said little about sexual sin specifically, the rest of the Word of God says plenty and **JESUS IS THE WORD!**

In the beginning was the Word, and the Word was with God, and the Word was God. The same was in the beginning with God. All things were made by him; and without him was not anything made that was made. In him was life; and the life was the light of men.

(John 1:1-4)

Nevertheless let me further clarify by saying this; the word "homosexual" is just another name-tag that people use; whereas "fornication" identifies the *sin* and *spiritual-influence* that's behind certain sexual behaviour. SO IF JESUS DID NOT FOCUS ON "NAME CALLING" OR "FINGER-POINTING" BUT THE "ROOT" OF THE ISSUE THEN WE MUST DO LIKEWISE. I ALWAYS REPEAT: IT'S NOT A GAY ISSUE BUT A SIN ISSUE.

All of us must continually submit our sexuality back to God, trusting Him. As most of us have found out the hard way that *all flesh* is corrupt *(even our own)* without Christ.

"Therefore let anyone who thinks he stands [who feels sure that he has a steadfast mind and is standing firm], take heed lest he fall [into sin]" (1 Corinthians 10:12 AMP). What a warning for all of us, to handle all such issues with a deep sense of humility *(not false humility)*.

The fact that none of us are "immune" is a point that is brought out brilliantly by "The Message" translation of the bible, *"...we are just as capable of messing it up as they were. Don't be so naive and self-confident. You're not exempt. You could fall flat on your face as easily as anyone else. Forget about self-confidence; it's useless. Cultivate God-confidence"* (1 Corinthians 10:12).

We saw this point brought out clearly in previous chapters within this book, that some folks, who are outraged by *sensitive* or *controversial* issues, are sometimes the biggest offenders! So let us not fall into the same chasm of hypocrisy. As I keep saying - we are all sexual and all capable of sexual vice - regardless of orientation or name tagging. It is all just one big deception of the enemy to *distort* and *pervert* our God given reality!

> **<u>Sexually confused,</u> they abused and defiled one another,** *women with women, men with men - all lust, no love.*
>
> *(Romans 1:26-27 MSG)*

So it is certain then that a vast amount of **sexual and emotional confusion** exists today, mainly due to the fact that people are essentially *disconnected* from God. They have lost their "natural affection" one to another but also their true spiritual and eternal identity. In addition ANYTHING OUTSIDE OF ITS "ORIGINAL ORDER" WILL FAIL ITS "ORIGINAL DESIGN."

The following is part of an article called **"Gay Activist Lied"** written by Stephen Green of **Christian Voice UK.**

"A Christian therapist faces discipline from her professional organization after a homosexual activist encouraged her to offer him therapy to become heterosexual. Patrick Strudwick, a journalist honoured of gays for his 'investigative' work, approached Lesley Pilkington at a Christian conference run by the National Association for Research and Therapy of Homosexuality. Strudwick told Mrs Pilkington that he was unhappy with his homosexual lifestyle and that he 'wanted to leave it.'

He then requested *'treatment for his same-sex attraction.'* After two sessions, which Strudwick recorded, he unveiled himself as a fraud to Mrs Pilkington and reported her to her professional body, the British Association for Counselling and Psychotherapy *(BACP).* The <u>BACP</u>, whose chief executive is Laurie Clarke, have summoned Mrs Pilkington to a disciplinary hearing on Thursday 20th January 2010 at a hotel in Rugby. She is being represented by leading human rights counsel Paul Diamond.

Christian Voice understands that BACP have refused to call three witnesses who have been delivered from homosexual desires by Christian-informed therapy and they have also refused to hear Dr Dean Bird, an American expert who is coming over for the case. In law, to refuse to hear a witness is to accept his written evidence, but it is unsure to what extent the BACP hearing, which is to be held in secret, will adhere to established principles of natural justice.

The fact is that the witnesses are living proof that Sexual Orientation Change Efforts *(SOCE)* is a proven therapy. What the gay lobby hates is that it works. And because it works, it exposes the foundation of the homosexual movement, that everyone is *'born like it,'* as a lie.

That is why homosexual activists want to stop the whole treatment, and why they want to bulldoze the BACP into ruling that patient autonomy, that *sacred cow* of psychotherapy, is not to be respected when a homosexual presents himself *(or herself)* as wanting to change. Strudwick told The Sunday Telegraph: 'If a black person goes to a GP and says I want skin bleaching treatment that does not put the onus on the practitioner to deliver the demands of the patient. It puts the onus on the health care practitioner to behave responsibly.'

But being black is immutable. It is not behaviour. No one *(except Michael Jackson)* has changed his skin colour from black to white, but thousands of homosexuals have become heterosexual. Of course, to develop Strudwick's argument, if a transsexual goes to a doctor asking for hormones and a gender-change operation to change sex, to quote Strudwick, 'the onus *(is)* on the health care practitioner to behave responsibly' and refer that person to a psychiatrist to get his head sorted out. That rarely happens. **Patient autonomy is respected in those cases to the point of expensive evil with surgeons mutilating the patient's God-given body.**

The Royal College of Psychiatrists buried its own head in the sand last year with a policy statement, which condemned conversion therapies. It stated: 'there is no sound scientific evidence that sexual orientation can be exchanged. Furthermore, so-called treatments of homosexuality create a setting in which prejudice and discrimination flourish.'

That was an obvious *politically correct* point. Not many know that the psychiatry profession was targeted by gay activists in the 1970s and browbeaten into changing its stance on homosexuality, which up to then had been regarded as an **objective disorder.** See this attack on SOCE by the American Psychological Association, this convincing reply by NARTH and this round up by Fulcrum-Anglican. **It was not evidence that changed the position of the profession, it was naked aggression. As a result, psychiatry is now riddled with non-sequiturs and logical absurdities.**

For example, the self-satisfied-to-the-point-of-smug 'agony uncle' Philip Hodson, a fellow of the BACP, said: '[BACP] is dedicated to social diversity, equality and inclusivity of treatment without sexual discrimination or judgmentalism of any kind, and it would be absurd to attempt to alter such fundamental aspects of personal identity as sexual orientation by counselling.'

Really? **Paedophilia and bestiality** are *sexual orientations.* Should psychiatrists not attempt to alter those fundamental aspects of personal identity either? What about other fundamental aspects of personal identity? Violence or theft, or sexual predation, perhaps? Of course, Lesley Pilkington is adamant that she is not passing judgment on those who come to her, and that is a sound professional position to take.

Nevertheless, for the rest of us, is there not a time when we have to say 'such and such a thing is wrong?' **In Christian Voice we are bold and *politically-incorrect* enough to say that pressing the rectum into service as a sexual organ is wrong, dirty, unhealthy and pathological.** And we also say that a homosexual lifestyle means living the lie that sodomy *(now politely called 'anal intercourse')* is the moral equivalent of heterosexual love and marriage.

Living a lie has a habit of expanding into the rest of life, until it becomes impossible to distinguish truth from falsehood, and lying becomes just part of what you do and who you are. Patrick Strudwick is living proof of that." *(This article was taken from Christian Voice/Jan 2011 -* http://www.christianvision.com. *National Director: Stephen Green. Similar article also found at this link:* http://www.telegraph.co.uk/news/uknews/8261705/The-therapist-who-claims-she-can-help-gay-men-go-straight.html*)*

In closing this chapter, I dare say that while the whole world is seemingly in confusion about this issue the bible is clearly NOT!

In fact the following scriptures could not be clearer! Take for instance the Old Testament in Leviticus 18:22 where it says *"Do not lie with a man as one lies with a woman; that is detestable" (NIV).* Or in the New Testament where it reads,

For this reason God gave them over and abandoned them to vile affections and degrading passions. For their women exchanged their natural function for an <u>unnatural</u> and <u>abnormal</u> one, And the men also turned from natural relations with women and were <u>set ablaze</u> (burning out, <u>consumed) with lust</u> for one another -- men committing shameful acts with men and suffering in their own bodies and personalities the inevitable consequences and penalty of their wrong-doing and going astray, which was [their] fitting retribution.

(Romans 1:26-27 AMP)

❖

CHAPTER 11

The Struggle can be Overcome

W hat a journey this has been! I have used this particular chapter to wrap up a very wide subject so let's continue right where we left off.

Now, the effects of the corrupt nature are obvious: illicit sex, perversion, promiscuity... drunkenness, wild partying... people who do things like that will not inherit the kingdom of God.

(Galatians 5:19-26 GW)

Now homosexuality exists within the Church as well as outside of the Church and there are those today who are still prepared to stand up in the face of this growing tide and speak God's Word directly at it! Over the years such people like Ulf Ekman have taken a more "militant" approach to homosexuality and been controversially very out spoken about the bible's stance towards homosexuality.

I have chosen to add an excerpt here from Ulf as he shares about a period in his life where he was studying to become a priest in Uppsala, Sweden. He writes: "One of the professors invited a number of homosexuals - Christian homosexuals - as they referred to themselves. They were asked to talk about the positive aspects of homosexuality to a group of between 200-300 prospective priests. A small group of us knew that they were coming, so we took some time that morning to pray.

We took authority over the spiritual forces, which lie behind homosexuality... This section of our education was nothing other than the seduction of future priests to accept homosexuality as a genuine form of love. It was then hoped that they would go on to spread that opinion in churches throughout the country.

However, homosexuality is not a genuine display or expression of love. According to the Word of God, it is an abomination in the eyes of God. Of course, just as with every other abomination, **it is possible to be delivered from homosexuality.** The blood of Jesus cleanses from all sin, when this sin is confessed. If evil spirits are involved, they can be cast out and the person can be set free."

Ulf Ekman went on to say, "The moment I set foot in the room, I noticed that for some reason the professor looked slightly shaken. He was upset and grumpy. It was obvious that the spirit powers, which we had bound, were now disturbed. **This group of five homosexuals began to talk about how 'fantastic' it was to be a homosexual and just how Christian it was.**

Afterwards we had the opportunity to ask questions. I was given the floor, so I turned to the first chapter of Romans and read what it says there about homosexuality. Then I said, 'You say that homosexuality is talked about only in the Old Testament and that the New Testament has nothing to say about it, but just seems to accept it. But here in Romans 1:27 is the same word which is used in Leviticus 18:22; the word 'abomination.' **The Word of God says that it is not at all acceptable, but that it is an abomination.**

I did not raise my voice or shout or prophesy; I just spoke calmly, led by the Holy Spirit. When I said this, the entire auditorium exploded. The Word of God came into the room like a hammer. The otherwise cultivated, aesthetic, humane, humanistic professor had suddenly become a different man. What was really inside him suddenly came out; he became angry and irritated... Their intention had been to come and neatly seduce us all, but now their plans had come to nothing. I did not stand up and say, *'Thus says the Lord,'* but said, *'I'd like to read a scripture.'* This scripture acted as a spear, a sword and a lance, which caused total chaos.

The professor completely lost his head and several others turned too and shouted, *'How lacking in love!'* This treachery is taking place today in schools, companies and within political debates, not just regarding homosexuality, but also the New Age movement and occultism. **Wherever you look**

you will discover this 'sophisticated' form of seduction. Some Christians have even become so sophisticated that they too have swallowed these things. It is time that we stood up and kicked the devil out of every single area where he has found an entrance."

Pastor Ekman concludes: "There is no reason why we should have to follow the devil's rules. God plays according to different rules. If the devil presents himself politely, intellectually and seductively, you can prophecy in the broadest dialect and say, *'Thus says the Lord!'* **God looks at the heart! God is looking for prophets who will prophesy in the Holy Spirit and not just run around getting angry at people or with no more than personal opinions to shout about everything"** *(The Prophetic Ministry, p172-176).*

Homosexuality is not a male phenomenon and we have already discussed at length, the intense nature of *promiscuity* that has risen up amongst females today *(of all ages).*

Scripture tells us that women also abandon their "natural affections." However *(whether in the church or in the secular world)* the *feminisation* of men and the *masculinisation* of women is all part of the distortion that Satan wants to create. Even when said in reverse, it means the same thing - the *emasculation* of men and the *defeminising* of women!

As a side issue, it's interesting that a popular online magazine brought to my attention just recently, is blatantly called **"Jezebel"** http://jezebel.com When I checked it out for myself I found that it was such a fitting title for a *rag* that promotes: *promiscuity, immorality and scorn.* Then again most secular magazines do!

One recent article even targeted Pastor Rick Warren entitled: "This Time Rick Warren Is Late to the Birth Control Outrage Game," alternatively another called, "God Thinks You Could Stand to Lose a Few Pounds" showing a less than flattering picture of Pastor Rick. Needless to say it's just like Jezebel to target men of God. **So no surprises there!** http:// jezebel.com/5884884/this-time-rick-warren-is-late-to-the-birth-control-outrage-game?tag=pill-baby-pill

However perhaps "Lilith" is even more insidious than Jezebel. A movement that seeks to bolster the feminist agenda through gatherings such as "Lilith Fair" www.lilithfair.com which showcases major international talent, particularly female musicians, while raising substantial funds for charity in the process.

The Fair was initially founded by talented musician Sarah McLachlan *(a professing "lesbian" at the time, who has since changed her status! I guess she was not "born-that-way!")* Anyhow most people are oblivious to this early Jewish *myth* about "Lilith," which was the name for Adam's first wife! As the myth goes, she had to have been the world's first *(rebellious)* woman!

Basically this ancient myth holds the notion that Lilith was created before Eve, she left Adam because she could no longer submit to him! Needless to say Lilith now represents strong women everywhere who hate ALL MALE AUTHORITY including and in particular - *God's!*

To continue however, while the story of Lilith might sound a truly crazy notion indeed, it is still most definitely being utilized to bolster the feminist agenda as we have said already but also by various Neo-Pagan groups and the New Agers.

At this point I would like to add an interesting excerpt from an interview with **"Marilyn Manson"** *(Satanist/ musician)* who offered his support of the "Lilith Fair" event from its inception. During an interview with MTV in 1997 he is famously quoted as saying:

> *I think the Lilith Fair was far more subversive and satanic than anything that I could have done because here you have people playing this very innocuous folk music that's providing America with love and very dangerous ideas about women's sexuality. <u>And I think a lot of Christians would be upset if they knew!</u>*

This is the same individual who notoriously "ranted" to a mass audience during MTV's Video music awards that same year: **"We will no longer be oppressed by the fascism of Christianity!"** Evidently, this feminist agenda features large on the map and is a key element in Satan's strategy to wage war on human sexuality. http://www.neverisapromise. com/interviews/MTVYRock.html

If you enjoy art like my wife and I do, you might know of Dante Gabriel Rossetti who was a member of the "Pre-Raphaelite Brotherhood" *(consisting of four English painters who formed a secret society in the 19th century. They pursued what they considered the "sincerities" of the early renaissance period - before Raphael - hence the term pre-Raphaelite!)*

During this time we know that Lilith as a myth had not faded out of people's minds, but was "alive-and-well" in the consciousness of the Victorians, as seen in Dante's painting famously called *"Lady Lilith!" (To see this painting go to* http://en.wikipedia.org/wiki/File:Lady-Lilith.jpg.*)*

Lilith was described in Judaic literature not only as the first wife of Adam and **the seducer of men** but was also interestingly associated with **the murder of children.** At this point I can interject that the sexual abuse of children has never just been a male dominated phenomenon; there are **female paedophiles** existing out there. In fact quite recently there have been high profile cases in the media, of nursery workers convicted of child sex abuse - as female paedophiles.

Even "paedo-couples" exist - where both partners selfishly engage in the act of molesting and videotaping their own children. **Once again, sexual sin is not a "male" problem but a "human" problem.**

Nevertheless Dante's depiction of Lilith was not as a paedophile, but as a powerful and evil temptress *(a prevalent theme in 19th-century painting, particularly among the Pre-Raphaelites).*

Well before this however was the Renaissance period that saw the ushering in of Secularism, Secular Humanism and the like; *(a transition period between the 14th-17th centuries)* that brought a greater emphasis on **non-religious** values. Evidenced mostly in the arts of this period, that featured "man-apart-from-God" type themes.

The word Renaissance itself means, "re-birth" and signified a wide spread "revival" of the arts, literature and all forms of study and learning *(that was strictly outside the confines of religion and the church!)*

In fact many of the early paintings from the renaissance involved much nudity and immorality - and perhaps most notably - many of the "Popes" commissioned and patronized *(funded)* such arts!

Actually it could be said that the early renaissance poets and artists wanted to study "any" subject that had as little, if anything to do with God, Jesus or the Church at all! They preferred instead to employ any number of *mythologies, philosophies and paganisms* - as topics for their work; **specifically and including the** *male nude.*

Actually Florence is considered the "birthplace" of the Renaissance, and as one of the wealthiest cities of the time; it both housed and funded much of its famous arts *(mainly via the powerful Medici family)*. But it's important to add here that Florence as a city was also famous for its immorality, particularly "sodomy" - which lent to the fact that much of its art work involved "the naked male form" *(most famously Michael Angelo's statue of "David")*. In other words the renaissance had its preoccupations with sodomy and controversy - its birthplace was Florence, Italy.

Evidently then, *every* generation has had its "seductions" to deal with, due to the "human condition" it matters little which geographical location, time in history, political agenda or climate existed at that time - as the sins involved are the same!

As for this generation things continue to change, both for the better and for the worse. And to bring things right back to the contemporary moment, I recently turned on my computer to watch the evening news and saw a segment concerning hotels, which briefly said; **"Many hotels are now declaring themselves *'Gay Friendly'* but are they really or are they just chasing the lucrative *Pink-Pound?"* (BBC World News, Live Station, Dec 2010).** This led me to take a closer look into what the markets are saying about this now illustrious "Pink-Pound," knowing that whatever affects the economy - affects all of us!

In today's world, nothing is considered "news-worthy" *unless* it affects the economy! Which is precisely why the gay movement is growing in influence and receiving more attention - because it is now affecting the economy on a much larger scale! According to **marketingweek.co.uk,** "The concept of the 'pink pound' has been in use since the Nineties, but it is only in recent times that this market has moved into the mainstream.

Brands such as Lloyds TSB, Ikea, Pepsi and Heinz have all launched campaigns that appeal to a gay audience." *(Occasionally, the similarly termed "blue pound" is used specifically for lesbians - this adds new emphasis to the "colour-of-money!")* http://www.marketingweek.co.uk/pink-pounds-value-rises-in-mainstream-markets/3020077.article And/or http://en.wikipedia.org/wiki/Pink_money.

According to Nick Gadsby, *(associate director of research firm Lawes Consulting),* "**...the rise in gay civil partnerships, and the Liberal Democrats putting fully-fledged gay** marriage on their agenda, means gay families will become a more conventional part of British society."

He told a Westminster Forum in September: **"What you're going to see [in society] is a lot more gay couples settling down to a relatively traditional conservative life of shopping at Sainsbury's and trying to get their kids into the best school."** He goes on to say, "This means that marketers need to focus on becoming more inclusive in their messaging... The **pink pound** is being slightly diverted from the more fun aspects that are traditionally associated with gay culture."

He continues, "Indeed, a range of targeted services from mainstream brands have launched in the past few years **to meet an anticipated specialist need from the gay community."** Thomson Holidays' specialist **"Freedom"** is an example of this.

"Freedom offers a 'GayComfort' seal of approval on all the hotels it promotes on its site, which product manager Tommy Lynch says, **'allows us to choose hotels that are willing to take our training on board to help them better understand how to work with gay customers...** We wanted to do more than just advertising because people can be cynical about corporations becoming gay friendly.'"

So in all of this we can see very clearly that times indeed are changing, in more ways than one. Society as we have known it will be unrecognizable just decades from now! And I will use this as my final quote *(marketingweek.co.uk):* **Case studies - UK advertisements featuring gay characters:**

- **Ikea** promoted its catalogue in 2009 by depicting a man coming home to his flat to find his girlfriend cooking dinner for her new female partner, with the strap line: "It's change time."

- **Pepsi** aired an advert in 2008 that showed two men in a bar encouraging their friend to chat to a woman. The man drinks PepsiMAX to get confidence and walks past two women, one being model Kelly Brook, before approaching a man at the end of the bar.

- **Heinz** released an advert in 2008 showing a man making sandwiches for his two children and his male partner. The two men then kissed each other goodbye before going to work. Heinz withdrew the ad after receiving several complaints that it was "inappropriate." However, the brand's decision to pull the ad resulted in a boycott of the brand by both gay and straight people *(Source: Stonewall's guide on how to market to gay consumers)*.

In closing, there have been some who have asked me, "What is the eternal fate of someone who is gay?" To answer this I will allow scripture to speak for itself:

It is obvious what kind of life develops out of trying to get your own way all the time: repetitive, loveless, cheap sex; a stinking accumulation of mental and emotional garbage; frenzied and joyless grabs for happiness; trinket gods; magic-show religion; paranoid loneliness; cutthroat competition; all-consuming-yet-never-satisfied wants; a brutal temper; an impotence to love or be loved; divided homes and divided lives; small-minded and lopsided pursuits; the vicious habit of depersonalizing everyone into a rival; uncontrolled and uncontrollable addictions; ugly parodies of community.

I could go on. This isn't the first time I have warned you, you know. IF YOU USE YOUR FREEDOM THIS WAY, YOU WILL NOT INHERIT GOD'S KINGDOM.
(Galatians 5:19-26 MSG)

Lastly - for anyone who is finding the struggle and temptation of sexual sin utterly "over whelming," - take courage and be reminded that God is bigger and more powerful than it all.

Remember that those whom the Son sets FREE are "free-indeed!" There is always a way out, especially when there seems to be no way - there is "always" hope:

No test or temptation that comes your way is beyond the course of what others have had to face. All you need to remember is that God will never let you down; he'll never let you be pushed past your limit; he'll always be there to help you come through it.
(1 Corinthians 10:13 MSG)

Finally: English martyr and evangelical preacher John Bradford *(circa 1510-1555)* once coined a famous phrase that we have all come to know and respect:

"There but for the grace of God, goes John Bradford." It is believed that he said this in response to seeing criminals being led to the scaffold. **So let me encourage everyone of us today - to hold this same attitude of grace...**

"There but for the grace of God, go I..."

❖

Chapter 12

The Final Requirement

I have chosen to conclude this book with some teaching from **Rick Renner** that helps to bring closure to this vast subject; in his own articulate style and deep knowledge of the original languages. Hence he writes:

"We live in a day when moral standards have deteriorated. Things that were considered sinful and shameful one generation ago are now practiced in a widespread manner throughout the Church. Rather than acknowledge their sin and repent, believers try to justify their actions as they can continue in their deeds. But no matter how painstakingly Christians may try to dress up sin, God still sees it as sin and **hates** it.

When Paul begins his list of the works of the flesh, **he begins with the sexual sins of adultery, fornication, and**

uncleanness. The word 'adultery' and 'fornication' both come from the same Greek word - the word *porneia.* **This word includes all sexual activity outside of marriage - including both** *adultery* **and** *homosexuality.*

When referring to a woman who has committed *adultery,* the New Testament used the word *pornos.* This is the word for *a prostitute,* and it very vividly informs us that **a woman who has committed adultery has** *prostituted herself.* She may not have sold herself for money; perhaps she traded her heart, her body, or her emotions for romance, for emotional support, or for a variety of other things. **But regardless of why she did it, God says she has** *sold herself* **and entered into** *the sin of prostitution.*

Don't deceive yourself into thinking that this term refers only to a professional prostitute who walks the streets at night or who works in an escort service. This word *pornos* describes *any* woman who has committed *adultery.* It leaves no room for doubt that in God's view, a woman who commits adultery has fallen into the sin of prostitution. *She is a prostitute.* One may try to give a myriad of reasons or excuses to explain why the illicit relationship occurred, but the fact is, God views such a relationship as *an act of prostitution.*

When referring to a man who has committed *adultery,* the word *porneia* depicts *a man who has had sexual intercourse with a prostitute.* Although his emotions may try to tell him that he has found the sweetheart of his dreams, the Greek word *porneia* means *he has slept with a prostitute.* A person may try as hard as he can to put a different light on this subject, but this is how God sees it. **Whenever a man has** sexual relations with a woman who is not his wife, God says his action is equivalent to seeking a prostitute for a cheap and dirty thrill.

I must point out that the word *pornography* comes from this same Greek word. In fact, pornography is from the Greek word *pornos* (the same word used above for **an adulteress** or a **prostitute**) and from the word *grapho*, which means **to write**. Thus, *pornography* refers to **the writings or reflections about prostitution**. This means that when an individual meditates on the writings or the photography contained in pornography, it is the equivalent of committing *mental prostitution*. Such a definition sheds new light on what Jesus said in Matthew 5:28: *'But I say unto you, That whosoever looketh on a woman to lust after her hath committed adultery with her already in his heart.'*

What I have shared with you thus far is not my opinion; it is the actual meaning of the Greek word **'adultery'** that is used throughout the New Testament. **So how does this affect your view of someone who has committed adultery? If you have committed adultery, how does this affect your view of what you have done? And how does this affect your view of pornography?**

If you are reading the *King James Version* of the New Testament, the next word in the works of the flesh is **'fornication.'** However, this word does not appear in this text in the original Greek; it speaks only of *porneia*, the word discussed above, which includes all forms of sexual activity outside of marriage. In Greek, the next point that Paul lists is **'uncleanness.'**

The word **'uncleanness'** is the Greek word *akatharsia,* which is the word *kathairo* with the prefix *a* added. The word *kathairo* means *cleansed* or *pure,* but when the *a* is added to it the condition is reversed, making the object *dirty or unclean.* In the New Testament, this word refers to *lewd or unclean thoughts that eventually produce lewd or unclean actions.* As it is used in the Gospels and Paul's epistles, it strongly suggests that these actions begin in the mind as unclean thoughts before they manifest as unclean deeds.

In Mark 1:23 it says *'And there was in their synagogue a man with an unclean spirit.'* The Greek actually says that this man was **'gripped by the control of an unclean spirit.'** It seems this man had pondered on *lewd thoughts* for so long that he had thrown open the door for these thoughts to seize and control him, so that eventually he found himself **'in the clutch'** of an unclean spirit. Although the text doesn't explicitly say it, the usage of the word *akatharsia* makes one wonder whether or not this demon found entrance into this man's life because he allowed his mind to dwell on things that were forbidden.

Had he committed mental prostitution to such an extent that it opened the door for him to be completely controlled by spirits of uncleanness? The bible doesn't say exactly so, but the usage of the word *akatharsia* definitely makes this a possibility.

In Mark 5:2, we find another example of a man with an unclean spirit. It says, *'And when he was come out of the ship, immediately there met him out of the tombs a man with an unclean spirit.'* The word **'unclean'** is also the word *akatharsia.* Just as Mark 1:23 depicted the man in the synagogue as being 'gripped by the control of an unclean spirit,' this word could be translated exactly the same way in this verse.

In the first five chapters of Mark, we thus have two **very demonized individuals** whose demon- possessed condition seems to have begun with *impure, lewd, dirty thoughts,* since this is exactly what the Greek word *akatharsia* means that is used in both texts. Did Satan lure them into the pornography of unclean ideas or into adultery, and then build a stronghold of uncleanness so robust in their minds that he was able to eventually cause unclean actions to be manifested in their lives and thus completely control them?

Never forget that Paul told us, *'Know ye not, that to whom ye yield yourselves servants to obey, his servants ye are to whom ye obey' (Romans 6:16).* **Whatever you give your mind to will eventually be your master.** Was this the case with these two demon-possessed men in Mark 1:23 and Mark 5:2? I am not stating it emphatically, but the Greek suggests this very strongly. However, it should certainly make us want to take charge of our thought life and not allow uncleanness to have any place in our minds!

As Paul continues listing the works of the flesh, he next mentions **'lasciviousness.'** This strange word comes from the Greek word *aselgeia.* This Greek word describes **excess, but it primarily refers to the excessive consumption of food or wild, undisciplined living that is especially marked by unbridled sex.** The word *aselgeia* is listed as the principal sin of the cities of Sodom and Gomorrah *(see 2 Peter 2:6)* and the reason that God overthrew them.

It must be noted again that the word *aselgeia* also refers to **the excessive consumption of food.** This means that in God's mind, it is just as perverted to overindulge in food, as it is to engage in sinful sexual activities! *So how does this make you feel about overeating?*

All of the works of the flesh can be forgiven - but before forgiveness comes, **sin must be acknowledged.** This is why we must understand exactly what these words mean. Once sin is comprehended, it can then be repented of and confessed. *This is God's requirement.*

If you have fallen into any of these works of the flesh, ask the Holy Spirit to open your eyes to see these sins as He sees them. **Once you get a revelation of *His* perspective, you won't want to be the same!** You'll understand the grossness of sin in God's sight, and you will want to be changed!

Once you confess your sin, God will forgive you and you can move on with your life. If your actions have violated your spouse or anyone else, pray for God's mighty grace to be upon them to forgive you. Then begin to take whatever steps are necessary to make that relationship healthier than ever before.

Finally dear friend, God is with you, and He wants to change your life. Open your heart and let the Holy Spirit be your Helper. He wants to help you get clean, get free, and become morally strong and stable.

My Prayer

Lord, I thank You for opening my eyes to the truth about how You see these works of the flesh. Forgive me for being too tolerant of these areas in my life. Help me to see these fleshly works the way You see them and to detest them as much as You detest them. Teach me to hate sin! Show me how to say no to ungodliness and to yield my mind and my body as instruments of righteousness. After what You have shown me today, I never want to be the same! I pray this in Jesus' name!

I confess that I think clean thoughts and that I don't allow the devil to mess with my mind. My mind belongs to Jesus. It is filled with the Word of God. That Word renews my mind to think God's thoughts; therefore, Satan has no entrance into my mind or emotions to deceive me with thoughts of sin. I crucify my flesh, and I bring my body under the Lordship of Jesus Christ. I am no longer the servant of sin - I am the servant of righteousness! I declare this by faith in Jesus' name!"

❖

Bibliography

- Callaway, Ewen. <u>Porn in the USA: Conservatives are Biggest Consumers</u>. (article) New York, New York USA: Published by ABC News. Copyright © February 2009 www.abcnews.go.com

- Cocks, Jay, and Richard Stengel, and Dennis Worrell. <u>Rock is a Four Lettered Word</u>. (70) Tampa, Florida USA: Published by TIME Magazine. Copyright © Sep 30, 1985

- Criminal Defense Lawyer. <u>When is Sodomy Unlawful?</u> (article) Pleasanton, California USA: Published by Criminal Defense Lawyer. Copyright © 2012 www.criminaldefenselawyer.com

- Eady, Robert. <u>Satanism, Witchcraft and Church Feminists</u>. (article) London, England: Published by Christian Order. Copyright © February 1998 www.catholicculture.org

- Ekman, Ulf. <u>The Prophetic Ministry</u>. (172-176) Uppsala, Sweden: Published by Enbloms Grafiska. Copyright © 1990

- Green, Stephen. <u>Gay Activist Lied</u>. (article) Coleshill, England: Published by Christian Voice. Copyright © January 2011 www.christianvision.com

- Marrs, Wanda, and Texe Marrs. <u>New Age Lies to Women</u>. (57-60, 107, 143-145) Austin, Texas USA: Published by Living Truth Publishers. Copyright © 1989

- Prince, Derek. <u>Prophetic Guide to the End Times: Facing the Future without Fear</u>. (91-93) Grand Rapids, Michigan USA: Published by Chosen Books. Copyright © 2008

- Reisman, Judith. <u>Women in a Video Cage</u>. (54) Washington, DC USA: Published by United Press International

- Renner, Rick. <u>Sparkling Gems from the Greek: Adultery, Fornication, Uncleanness, Lasciviousness</u>. (article) Tulsa, Oklahoma USA: Published by Renner Ministries. Copyright © July 2009 www.renner.org

- Ropelato, Jerry. <u>Women and Pornography</u>. (article) Ogden, Utah USA: Published by Internet Pornography Statistics - Top Ten Reviews. Copyright © 2012 www.internet-filter-review.toptenreviews.com

- Strong, James. S.T.D., L.L.D. 1890. <u>Strong's Exhaustive Concordance; Dictionaries of the Hebrew and Greek Words</u>. e-Sword ® version 7.6.1 Copyright © 2000-2005. All Rights Reserved. Registered trade mark of Rick Meyers. Equipping Ministries Foundation. USA www.e-sword.net

- WND. <u>Pedophiles launch own Political Party</u>. (article) Washington, DC USA: Published by WND. Copyright © May 2006 www.wnd.com

- Unless otherwise indicated, all scriptural quotations are taken from the King James Version of the bible.

- Scripture quotations marked "AMP" are taken from The Amplified Bible. *Old Testament* copyright © 1965, 1987 by Zondervan Corporation, Grand Rapids, Michigan. *New Testament* copyright © 1958, 1987 by The Lockman Foundation, La Habra, California. All rights reserved.

- Scripture references marked "GW" are taken from GOD'S WORD®, © 1995 God's Word to the Nations. Used by permission of Baker Publishing Group.

- Scripture references marked "MSG" are taken from The Message. Copyright © 1993, 1994, 1995, 1996, 2000, 2001, 2002. Used by permission of NavPress Publishing Group.

Bibliography

- Scripture references marked "NIV" are from the HOLY BIBLE, NEW INTERNATIONAL VERSION®. NIV®. Copyright © 1973, 1978, 1984 by the International Bible Society. Used by permission of Zondervan Publishing House. All rights reserved.

- Scripture quotations marked "NLT" are taken from the Holy Bible, New Living Translation, copyright © 1996, 2004, 2007 by Tyndale House Foundation. Used by permission of Tyndale House Publishers, Inc., Carol Stream, Illinois 60188. All rights reserved.

❖

Recommended Reading

- Cole, Edwin Louis, and Nancy Cole. <u>The Unique Woman</u>. Tulsa, Oklahoma USA: Published by Honor Books. Copyright © 1991

- Cole, Edwin Louis. <u>Maximized Manhood</u>. New Kensington, Pennsylvania USA: Published by Whitaker House. Copyright © 1982

- Cooper, Darien B. <u>You Can Be the Wife of a Happy Husband</u>. New Shippensburg, Pennsylvania USA: Published by Destiny Image. Copyright © 2011

❖

Ministry Profile - Dr Alan

Doctor Alan Pateman, an apostle, is the President and Founder of **"Alan Pateman Ministries International"** (APMI), which was established in England back in 1987, a Christian-based *(parachurch)* non-profit and non-denominational outreach. This ministry is now focusing in two main areas: First **"Connecting for Excellence"** Apostolic Networking (CFE) and secondly, the teaching arm, **"LifeStyle International Christian University"** (LICU).

CFE is a multi-facetted missions organisation with the purpose of connecting leaders for divine opportunities and building lasting relationships, to touch the lives of leaders literally the world over. Apostle Dr Alan Pateman has to date ordained more than 500 ministers in over 50 NATIONS. In addition there are ministries, churches and schools who are in Association or Affiliation, looking to him for apostolic counsel and oversight.

Secondly LICU, which was founded in 2007, is a study program to help people discover their purpose and destiny. A global network of university campuses and correspondence students, demonstrating the Supernatural Kingdom of God through Doctrinal, Apostolic and Prophetic Teaching. Dr Alan holds the position of President/CEO, Professor of Theology, Biblical Studies and Apostolic Ministry. LICU is exploding throughout Europe, Asia and Africa, enhancing the Body of Christ

Dr Alan has authored more than 35 books including numerous teaching materials and LICU university courses (30) along with hundreds of Truth for the Journey articles on kingdom lifestyle *(that are regularly distributed globally via the internet)*.

He is recognised as an Apostle, Bishop, Leadership Mentor, University Educator, Motivational Speaker, Connector and Author, who has also been featured on national and international TV and radio networks throughout the years.

Currently Apostle Alan, his wife Dr Jennifer reside in Lucca *(Tuscany)* Italy and travel out from their Apostolic Company.

- Alan Pateman Ph.D., D.Min., D.D., M.A., B.Th.

Academic Background

Dr. Alan Pateman attended several colleges throughout his training *(including studying Theology at Roffey Place, Horsham, UK and a Member of Kerygma - with Rev. Colin Urquhart and Dr. Bob Gordon - 1985-1987)* before being awarded a Doctorate of Divinity *(2006)* in recognition of his lifetime achievements by the International College of Excellence, now "DanEl Christian College" *(President: Dr. Robb Thompson USA)* also "Life Christian University" *(Dr. Douglas Wingate USA)* where he also earned a Bachelor of Theology B.Th. *(2006)*, a Master of Arts in Theology M.A., a Doctor of Ministry in Theology D.Min., *(2007)* and Doctor of Philosophy in Theology Ph.D. *(2013)* from LICU.

❖

Ministry Profile - Dr Jennifer

Apostle Doctor Jennifer Pateman's passion is to see the Body of Christ equipped and walking in spiritually maturity, through a married dependency on God's Spirit and Word. Her teaching ministry has a distinct prophetic flavour and she desires to see people of all ages succeed in their God given lanes.

Officially Jennifer is the Vice President of **Alan Pateman Ministries** (APMI) and Co-Founder of **Connecting for Excellence** (CFE) and **LifeStyle International Christian University** (LICU). She is a five-fold teaching gift to the Body of Christ, author, musician, public speaker, lecturer and researcher. Apart from travelling internationally alongside her husband, she is also on the Board of Executives and functions as the Executive Dean of LICU; also holding the position of Professor of Theology, Biblical Studies, and Pastoral Ministry.

Most importantly Dr Jennifer is devoted to her Man of God and three beautiful children; they reside in Lucca, Italy and travel out from their Apostolic Company.

- Jennifer Pateman Ph.D., D.Min., D.D., M.A., B.Th.

Academic Background

Dr. Jennifer Pateman has gained her Bachelor of Christian Theology B.Th., Master of Arts in Christian Theology M.A., Doctor of Divinity D.D., Doctor of Ministry D.Min., Doctor of Philosophy in Theology Ph.D. via the following institutes: International College of Excellence *(USA, Principal Dr. Robb Thompson)*, Life Christian University *(USA, Principal Dr. Douglas Wingate)*, LifeStyle International Christian University.

❖

To Contact the Authors

Please email:

Alan Pateman Ministries International

Email: apostledr@alanpateman.com
Email: drjennifer@alanpatemanministries.com
Web: www.AlanPatemanMinistries.com

*Please include your prayer requests
and comments when you write.*

❖

Other Books

Media, Spiritual Gateway

Let's face it; we live in the era of fake news! It's always existed, but never been quite so prominent. Today it's an all-out-war between fact and political fiction.

ISBN: 978-1-909132-54-2, Pages: 192, Format: Paperback, Published: 2018
Also available in eBook format!

Millennial Myopia, From a Biblical Perspective

The standard for every generation is Jesus. However Millennial Myopia describes the trap of focusing everything on one particular generation or demographic cohort, at the exclusion and expense of all others. The Church cannot afford to make this mistake too.

ISBN: 978-1-909132-67-2, Pages: 216, Format: Paperback, Published: 2017
Also available in eBook format!

Truth for the Journey Books

TONGUES, Our Supernatural Prayer Language

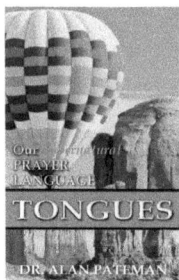

In writing to the church at Corinth, Paul encouraged them to continue the practice of speaking with other tongues in their worship of God and in their prayer lives as a means of spiritual edification. "He that speaketh in an unknown tongue edifies, charges, builds himself up like a battery."

ISBN: 978-1-909132-44-3, Pages: 144,
Format: Paperback, Published: 2016
Also available in eBook format!

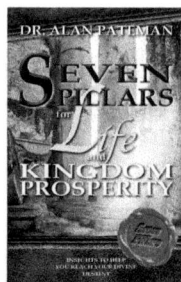

Seven Pillars for Life and Kingdom Prosperity

I submit these "Seven Pillars for Life and Kingdom Prosperity" to you, (Love, Prayer, Righteousness, Obedience, Connections, Management, Money). It's my desire that you walk in the triumphs that God has ordained for you.

ISBN: 978-1-909132-46-7, Pages: 220,
Format: Paperback, Published: 2016
Also available in eBook format!

Seduction & Control: Infiltrating Society & the Church

This book is a glance into the world of seduction and control, how they try to influence the Church through many powerful avenues such as the New Age, sexual education in our schools, basic entertainment; things that touch our everyday lives in order that we effectively and gradually become desensitised.

ISBN: 978-1-909132-00-9, Pages: 156
Format: Paperback, Published: 2015
Also available in eBook format!

Truth for the Journey Books

Kingdom Management for Anointed Prosperity

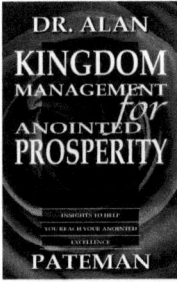

In his book, "Kingdom Management for Anointed Prosperity," Dr. Alan Pateman reveals how we can avoid living in continual crisis due to mismanagement. Life happens to all of us, but how we handle it matters most.

ISBN: 978-1-909132-34-4, Pages: 144,
Format: Paperback, Published: 2015
Also available in eBook format!

Why War: A Biblical Approach to the Armour of God and Spiritual Warfare

Spiritual warfare means different things to different people, but from a biblical standpoint Ephesians 6:10-18 gives us the best biblical definition of spiritual warfare possible. We can also see how God has thoroughly equipped us for victory not just self defence!

ISBN: 978-1-909132-39-9, Pages: 180,
Format: Paperback, Published: 2013
Also available in eBook format!

Forgiveness, The Key to Revival

Scripture is absolute when it comes to forgiveness. IF we forgive, THEN we are forgiven. It's that simple but no one said it was easy! Nonetheless, forgiveness can be likened to a spiritual key that unlocks spiritual doors and opportunities!

ISBN: 978-1-909132-41-2, Pages: 124,
Format: Paperback, Published: 2013
Also available in eBook format!

Truth for the Journey Books

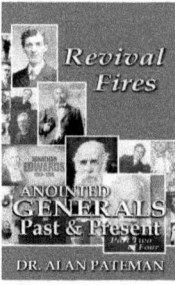

Revival Fires - Anointed Generals
Past & Present (Part Two of Four)

Seasons might be changing but God's Word remains the same. The heart of the author is to help train, equip and be a blessing to those men and women who will be willing to fulfil their potential in ministry and be properly equipped for service.

ISBN: 978-1-909132-36-8, Pages: 142,
Format: Paperback, Published: 2012
Also available in eBook format!

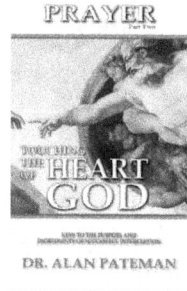

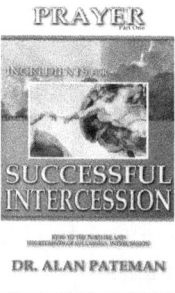

Prayer, Touching the Heart of God (Part Two)

Touching the Heart of God is the very essence of prayer. Whether we are petitioning God with very specific requests or consecrating ourselves before Him and rededicating our lives - whatever the case may be – the true essence of all praying is "Touching the Heart of God."

ISBN: 978-1-909132-12-2, Pages: 180,
Format: Paperback, Published: 2012
Also available in eBook format!

Prayer, Ingredients for Successful Intercession
(Part One)

This Book is the first of two books on Prayer. Dr. Pateman provides an exhaustive study, showcasing the vital ingredients necessary for all successful prayer. An excellent power-packed teaching tool, either for the individual or for the local church prayer group, that's eager to lay a solid foundation but don't know where to start!

ISBN: 978-1-909132-11-5, Pages: 140,
Format: Paperback, Published: 2012
Also available in eBook format!

Truth for the Journey Books

Apostles: Can the Church Survive Without Them?

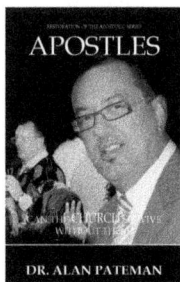

Before Jesus returns a significant increase of the anointing will be poured out on the Body of Christ, but can the Church handle such an anointing? *(Acts 5:5)* Billy Brim once said, "As much as the anointing is powerful to create, it is as powerfully destructive of evil." The fear of God will be restored with the apostolic and people will begin walking with such anointing, as we have never seen before!

ISBN: 978-1-909132-04-7, Pages: 164,
Format: Paperback, Published: 2012
Also available in eBook format!

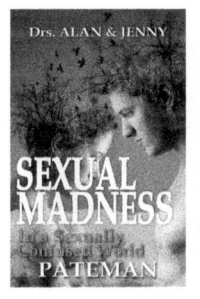

Sexual Madness: In a Sexually Confused World

This book discusses the sensitive subject of political correctness in our world today and the growing fear of causing offence in the public arena. It also discusses the rise of homosexuality, pedophilia and all other forms of sexuality, as there are many. Including modern statistics on pornography.

ISBN: 978-1-909132-02-3, Pages: 160,
Format: Paperback, Published: 2012
Also available in eBook format!

His Life is in the Blood

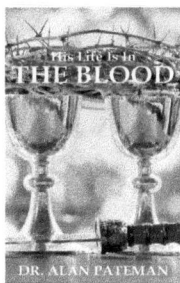

Blood is the trophy of every battle. The spilt blood of Jesus Christ is our trophy. It is our freedom from sin and bondage. Nothing can enter the blood-bought temples of the Holy Ghost! This book will encourage you to apply the blood of Jesus our Passover Lamb to your life, just as the children of Israel did in the Old Testament. Not merely talking or reading about it, but applying it.

ISBN: 978-1-909132-06-1, Pages: 152,
Format: Paperback, First Published: 2007
Also available in eBook format!

Truth for the Journey Books

WINNING by Mastering your Mind

Someone once said, "Happiness begins between your ears and your mind is the drawing room for tomorrow's circumstances..." Remember, what happens in your mind will happen in time, and therefore one of our first priorities must be mind-management.

ISBN: 978-1-909132-40-5, Pages: 136, Format: Paperback, Published: 2017
Also available in eBook format!

LIFESTYLE UNIVERSITY

Raising Up
Christian Leaders

Dear Friends,

Have you considered becoming one of our international students? We are privileged to welcome you, from around the world, to "LifeStyle International Christian University" *(the teaching arm of Alan Pateman Ministries International)*. **An English speaking university** dedicated to your success; to see you trained and equipped to fully succeed in your God given Destiny.

It is our passion to raise up the leaders of tomorrow, who will have influence in all realms of authority, including the Body of Christ. Men and women of strategy, wisdom and true godliness, who'll stand with stature and maturity in this hour.

It's undeniable that in today's world, recognised education has become indispensable, therefore it is our desire to offer well balanced and well structured courses. Those that have been written by gifted and talented ministers of God, who seek to be inspired by God's Holy Spirit.

Consequently we have put together a **flexible curriculum,** designed both for correspondence students and campuses, which is a strategy to reach the distant learner; whether provincial, national or international. In fact we have many correspondence students from around the world, including a growing number of successful campuses, in various countries.

This is a growing platform, where men and women of dignity and passion, can grow and be established in their God given endeavours. As God is the healer of the nations, we pray and believe that many of our alumni will go on to **become world changers** in their own right.

We are proud of each and every one of our LICU students.
It would be our pleasure if you would join them on this incredible journey!

Doctor Alan Pateman

Alan Pateman Prof. Ph.D., D.Min., D.D., M.A., B.Th.
PRESIDENT AND CEO
www.licuuniversity.com   www.cfeapostolicnetwork.com
Email: info@licuuniversity.com   Mob: +39 366 329 1315

For more information visit our website/facebook or contact our office, using the details below:

Website: www.licuuniversity.com
Facebook: www.facebook.com/LICUMainCampus
Email: info@licuuniversity.com
Telephone: +39 366 329 1315

ALAN PATEMAN MINISTRIES
PRESENTS

TEACHING - LEARNING - LIVING

A MASTER CLASS
with Dr Alan Pateman

DR. ALAN IS AVAILABLE
TO HOLD TEACHING
SEMINARS ON SATURDAYS
WITH YOUR LEADERS /
MEMBERS AND THEN
MINISTER AT YOUR
SUNDAY SERVICE.
PLEASE CONTACT OUR
OFFICE FOR AVAILABILITY.

OFFICE: VIA DEL GALLO, 18,
55100 LUCCA (LU), ITALY
TEL. 0039 366 329 1315
APOSTLEDR@ALANPATEMAN.COM

www.alanpatemanministries.com

All Books Available

at

APMI PUBLICATIONS

Email: publications@alanpateman.com
*Also Available from Amazon.com
and other retail outlets.*

*If you purchased this book through Amazon.com
or other and enjoyed reading it, or perhaps one of
my other books, I would be grateful if you could
take a couple of minutes to write a Customer
Review, many thanks.*

www.ingramcontent.com/pod-product-compliance
Lightning Source LLC
Chambersburg PA
CBHW071538040426
42452CB00008B/1062